VICTORIAN AND EDWARDIAN LOCOMOTIVE PORTRAITS

THE SOUTH OF ENGLAND

VICTORIAN AND EDWARDIAN LOCOMOTIVE PORTRAITS
THE SOUTH OF ENGLAND

Anthony Burton

PEN & SWORD
TRANSPORT

AN IMPRINT OF PEN & SWORD BOOKS LTD.
YORKSHIRE – PHILADELPHIA

First published in Great Britain in 2024 by
Pen and Sword Transport
An imprint of
Pen & Sword Books Ltd.
Yorkshire - Philadelphia

ISBN 978 1 39906 189 6

Typeset by SJmagic DESIGN SERVICES, India.
Printed and bound in India by Parksons Graphics Pvt. Ltd.

Pen & Sword Books Ltd. incorporates the imprints of Pen & Sword Books: After the Battle,
Archaeology, Atlas, Aviation, Battleground, Discovery, Family History, History, Maritime,
Military, Naval, Politics, Railways, Select, Transport, True Crime, Fiction, Frontline Books,
Leo Cooper, Praetorian Press, Seaforth Publishing, Wharncliffe and White Owl.

For a complete list of Pen & Sword titles please contact

PEN & SWORD BOOKS LIMITED
George House, Units 12 & 13, Beevor Street, Off Pontefract Road,
Barnsley, South Yorkshire, S71 1HN, England
E-mail: enquiries@pen-and-sword.co.uk
Website: www.pen-and-sword.co.uk

or

PEN AND SWORD BOOKS
1950 Lawrence Rd, Havertown, PA 19083, USA
E-mail: uspen-and-sword@casematepublishers.com
Website: www.penandswordbooks.com

Contents

Acknowledgements

The photographs used in this book are from the John Scott Morgan Collection, apart from the following: R.K. BLencowe, pp. 55, 62, 110, 118, 119, 120; Geoff D. Smith, Online Transport Archive, Guilford, 102, 103, 105, 1107, 108; GWR Official, 92; Hopwood Collection, 34, 35, 77; Online Transport Archive, RAS Collection, 70, 71, 72, 75, 82, 83, 108, 109, 125; Southern Railway Official, 51.

Every effort has been made to establish the identity of photographers and copyright holders where appropriate.

The author would also like to thank Niall Davitt for supplying extra research material.

CHAPTER ONE

Early Developments

For a quarter of a century, from 1804 when Richard Trevithick gave the first public demonstration of a steam locomotive running on rails on the Penydarren tramway in South Wales, development was limited to providing comparatively simple engines to be used exclusively for hauling freight, mostly coal. It is true that the Stockton & Darlington Railway, authorised in 1825, did run a limited passenger service, but it consisted of nothing more than a common stage coach, pulled by horses, only differing from the coaches in use on the roads by having flanged wheels. The first locomotive used on the line, *Locomotion*, was basic, with two cylinders in line, set into the boiler above the two drive axles, which itself had just a single flue. There were numerous problems. The spoked wheels proved fragile and as the engine ran on an uneven track and lacked springing, they often broke and were replaced later by solid plug wheels. The boiler proved inadequate, and it was often difficult to get up steam. On one day, the engine came to halt right on a busy road crossing and was only got going again by means of a hearty shove by the crossing keeper's wife.

It was only with the promotion of the Liverpool & Manchester Railway that the big question was asked. Could locomotives be powerful and fast enough to run a profitable passenger service alongside its goods business? Given the performance of *Locomotion* it is hardly surprising that there were many who doubted if that would be possible. There was a good deal of debate, with one camp arguing that the best solution would be to have a series of stationary steam engines, with coaches and trucks being hauled from one to the other by cables. Others were convinced that the locomotives would do the job better. The whole question was to be put to a practical trial on a straight section of the line at Rainhill in 1829. Engineers were invited to enter locomotives that had to meet specific conditions: four-wheeled engines had a weight limit of 4½ tons; six-wheeled, 6 tons; steam pressure was limited to 50 pounds per square inch (psi); and the six wheelers were expected to travel a distance equivalent to a return journey between Liverpool and Manchester hauling a 20 ton train at the rate of 10mph. Imperial units will be used throughout, as they were the ones in use at the time. The engine also had to 'consume their own smoke' – which, in practice, meant that they had to use coke instead of coal as the fuel. One other requirement was that a safety valve should be fitted, which the driver was unable to tamper with. This was sensible, as in the early days frustrated drivers had attempted to get more power from their engines by fastening down the safety. On the Stockton & Darlington this was common practice and on occasions when an engine was left stationary, it resulted in the fire tube collapsing. More dramatically, it could lead to a boiler explosion. Sadly, not all those who attempted this dangerous operation survived to learn from their mistake. The successful builders, if any met the requirements, were to receive a £500 prize and a contract to build locomotives for the line.

There were a number of hopeful entrants, but in the event there were only three serious contestants. One of them, *Novelty*, was a lightweight affair that never really got going. The old guard was represented by Timothy Hackworth's *Sans Pareil*. The locomotive was sturdy and, when a replica was built to celebrate the 150th anniversary of the event, proved to be a good and reliable locomotive. The original, however, suffered breakdowns on the day and, like *Novelty*, never completed the course. Although it was far more reliable than *Locomotion,* there was nothing that was really new or capable of greater development in the engine. Like other colliery engines of the time, it had a simple, return flue boiler, and vertical pistons driving the rear wheels. The other locomotive was *Rocket,* designed by Robert Stephenson and built at the Stephenson works in Newcastle. It had features that made it far more efficient than any of its predecessors. To increase the heat of the fire, exhaust steam was sent up the chimney via a blast

pipe, drawing air through the firebox. It was not a new idea – Trevithick had used it over twenty years earlier – but there is no great advantage in increasing the heat unless it can be used efficiently. The most radical feature of the locomotive was its boiler that used a design first suggested to Stephenson by Henry Booth, the railway company's treasurer. The hot gases from the firebox passed through twenty-five tubes running through the boiler itself, providing a far greater heating area than the simple return flue boiler. The third difference was in the position of the cylinders, inclined at an angle of 38 degrees, driving the front wheels. When the locomotive was put into service, it was modified by lowering the angle of the cylinders to an almost horizontal position at 8 degrees. These three features – blast pipe exhaust, multi-tubular boiler and steam cylinders at or near the horizontal – were to characterise locomotive development throughout the steam age. *Rocket* proved its worth at Rainhill, by hauling 42 tons at an average speed of 14mph on level track and then astonished the spectators by running light at an unprecedented 35mph.

The Liverpool & Manchester was unable to claim to offer the world's first steam powered passenger service. That honour went to the little Canterbury & Whitstable that opened in 1830, just pipping its more imposing rival to the post, but was actually run using a locomotive, *Invicta,* closely based on *Rocket* with the same sloping cylinders, but this time set at the opposite end of the boiler. The engine was also from the Stephenson factory, where work was going ahead building improved versions of *Rocket.* The obvious difference was an increase in the number of boiler tubes, at first to 88 then to 90, trebling

Robert Stephenson's *Rocket,* the forerunner of modern steam locomotives, had the three novel features of multi-tubular boiler, exhaust blast and angled cylinders. The engine now on display at the London Science Museum is the adapted version that went into service with the cylinders set at a lower angle than in the version that ran in the Rainhill Trials.

the surface area of the original and wheel size was increased from 4ft to 5ft diameter. The cylinders were also lowered to near horizontal. By the time the last of the series, *Northumbrian* and *Majestic*, had appeared, the locomotives had become even larger, weighing in at 8 tons, and cylinder size had increased from 8in bore and 17in stroke to 11in and 16in. The other major change was that where *Rocket* had a separate water-jacketed firebox, *Northumbrian* had one integrated into the boiler, another step that would be carried forward with later models.

The Stephenson works continued to develop the locomotive in the early years of the Liverpool & Manchester. The first new class to emerge was the Planet, first introduced in 1830. There were two very obvious differences. Firstly, the engine had a separate frame, where previously everything had been attached to the boiler. This consisted of wooden beams on each side of the engine, reinforced by iron plates on both sides, a 'sandwich frame'. Secondly, the cylinders had been moved inside the frame, driving onto a cranked axle. The engine also had a dome above the boiler, designed to keep the steam inlet well above the water level to make for dried steam in its passage from the boiler to the cylinders. Where *Rocket* had been fitted with oak tyres bound with iron, the Planets had hollow iron spokes fitted into cast iron rim and hub.

When the first steam railway in London, the London & Greenwich, received its Act in 1833, it was the most remarkable of all the early railways. Running for nearly 4 miles, it was carried on an immense viaduct of 878 brick arches. The locomotives used for the opening in 1836 were supplied by a variety of manufacturers but were basically all of the Planet type. The next railway in London was

equally bizarre. The London & Blackwall, designed to serve the docks, was originally planned by John Rennie, and he chose an odd gauge of 5ft ½in. However, when it came to construction, the chosen engineer was Robert Stephenson who, because of the gradient, opted for cable haulage by stationary steam engines. It opened in 1840 and was later converted for use by locomotives. It was later to be joined by the Eastern Countries Railway, also built originally to a 5ft gauge. The first passenger locomotives were 2-2-0s provided by Braithwaite, Milner & Co. The first named was John Braithwaite, who had been involved in the design of *Novelty* for the Rainhill trials. They were not considered satisfactory. The line was later converted to 4ft 8½in at Robert Stephenson's suggestion.

One of the problems faced by Stephenson on the earlier locomotives was the breaking of the crank axles. He believed that this was caused by the unequal pressure on the flanged drive wheels when going round curves. He patented the introduction of flangeless drive wheels, which he thought would solve the problems and in the same patent also described improved spoked wheels. The new ideas were incorporated into the Patentee class, larger than the Planets, with an additional pair of wheels beneath the firebox, making it a 2-2-2 instead of a 2-2-0. It was also the first to use steam brakes. Stephenson himself described the new brake, in plain, simple to understand language:

[It] consists in applying the force of small extra steam-pistons fitted into suitable cylinders, which by turning a cock can be supplied when required with steam from the boiler in order to act upon a double brake, or pair

Lion, one of half a dozen six-wheeled locomotives, designed by Robert Stephenson and built by Todd, Kitson & Laird for the Liverpool & Manchester in 1839. It demonstrates how far locomotive design had developed in the ten years after Rainhill.

of cogs, which are applied to the circumference of the of the said main-wheels without flanges and of the two additional small wheels.

There were serious competitors to Robert Stephenson in these early years. One was Edward Bury. He built two locomotives, *Dreadnought* and *Liverpool*, for the Liverpool & Manchester, though he owned them himself. They were, like the Planets, inside cylinder engines with cranked axles, but they had two sets of coupled driving wheels in an 0-4-0 arrangement. George Stephenson was not happy with the fact that the wheels were 6ft diameter as against the 5ft used on all the Stephenson engines. They originally used bellows for draught and had a convoluted tube arrangement but were later converted to multi-tube and exhaust blast. In this form, *Liverpool* was taken to the Bolton & Leigh where it worked satisfactorily for many years. Another major manufacturer was Sharp Roberts who, around 1837, introduced a modified outside frame that curved down on each side of the driving axle. They built 2-2-2s in which the drive wheels in the centre were larger than the other two sets of wheels. There was a large dome immediately behind the chimney. Altogether some 500 2-2-2 'Sharpies' had been built by the end of 1849.

Although we think of railways as being a product of Victorian Britain, all these developments took place before she arrived on the throne, but it was during these early years that the pattern was set that was to form the basis for later developments. By the time Victoria succeeded William IV in 1837, the network had already begun to spread. Scotland had its first lines with the Edinburgh & Dalkeith and the Dundee & Newtyle. There were isolated routes, such as the Leicester & Swannington and the Leeds & Selby, and the first Irish railway had opened, the Dublin to Kingstown. More importantly, there were new major routes, linking the Liverpool & Manchester to London, via the Grand Junction and the London & Birmingham. New companies meant new engineers and new engineering works, producing a rich variety of locomotives. All of these were built to the Stephenson gauge of 4ft 8½inches. One new company, however, took a very different view of how things should be done: the Great Western Railway (GWR), authorised in 1835.

The GWR engineer was, of course, Isambard Kingdom Brunel, who, after travelling on the Liverpool & Manchester, was unhappy with the uneven ride. The Stephenson gauge had not exactly been a deliberate choice. George Stephenson had been asked to build a locomotive for use on an old horse worked colliery line and when that did the job simply kept to the same gauge for every other line with which he was involved. Brunel took a different approach – what would be the most efficient track for a steam railway? He decided on a 7ft broad gauge, with a very rigid track laid on longitudinal wooden sleepers. Having decided on the perfect track for high-speed travel, he then had to decide on the design requirements for locomotives, and here boldness gave way to stultifying caution. He asked the builders to work towards a top speed of 30mph – a rate already achieved by *Rocket* though without a load. He then specified that piston speeds should be limited to 280ft per minute, though other locomotives were already working with speeds in excess of five hundred. Weight was to be limited to 6 tons on four wheels but go up to 10½ tons on six wheels. The builders were faced with almost irreconcilable demands: to get the 30mph with a low piston speed, they had to increase the size of the drive wheels to an unprecedented 6ft diameter. That inevitably increased the overall weight and as a result the boiler had to be reduced from the ideal size to compensate. There was a bizarre attempt to overcome the weight problem in two locomotives produced by Hawthorns of Newcastle, who mounted the boiler on a separate carriage, connected to the power unit by flexible hoses. They were not a success.

Brunel's dream of having the best service ever seen seemed doomed to failure and his reputation as one of the world's great engineers might have been lost for ever. Fortunately, he brought in a new engineer, Daniel Gooch, who had served an engineering apprenticeship and, at the age of just 19, joined the Stephenson works in Newcastle. Whilst there, he was able to work on a 6ft gauge locomotive being built for America, and was very impressed by the way in which the space between the wheels made it easier to 'arrange the engine'. This suggests that it was his shared enthusiasm for broad gauge that led him to Brunel. For some reason, the engines never went to America and Gooch persuaded Brunel to buy and adapt them to the 7ft gauge. The first to arrive was *North Star,* which may not have met Brunel's strict requirements, but proved to be the only really reliable locomotive on the line. The strange limitations originally imposed went to the scrap heap. The engine was, however, really a Patentee adapted to a different gauge.

Gooch took charge of the company's new locomotive works at Swindon. It was there that he developed the Firefly class of locomotives, all with a 2-2-2 arrangement, but with increasing power, a series of highly successful locomotive types of ever-increasing size and power, culminating in the *Great Western* of 1846. Weighing in at a hefty 29 tons, it proved to be too much to bear, and resulted in a broken leading axle. After that it was converted to a 4-2-2 and led on to the development of the Iron Duke class of 4-2-2s of which twenty-nine were built between 1847 and 1859 and which continued to work express trains until the broad gauge was dismantled in 1892. They must count as one of the most successful classes, in terms of longevity, of the Victorian era. The GWR was not the only British company to opt for a broad gauge. The first Irish railway, the Dublin & Kingstown, had been built to the Stephenson gauge. But the Ulster Railway, on the advice of the Railway Commissioners, was built to 6ft 2in. Then, just to complicate matters further, the Dublin & Drogheda went for a compromise that fitted neither and built their lines at 5ft 2in. Eventually, the authorities had to step in and set the standard gauge for Ireland at 5ft 3in – the Dublin & Kingstown was converted to the new measurement.

The broad gauge was an anomaly as the Stephenson gauge spread throughout the rest of Britain, bringing new companies and engineers with new ideas. The Grand Junction Railway that linked Birmingham to Warrington was opened in 1837 with Joseph Locke as the chief engineer. He established the company works at what was then no more than a hamlet at Crewe. He appointed William Buddicom as locomotive supervisor. The company had originally used Patentee locomotives, but Buddicom was not happy with the performance. In 1840, he introduced a new type of engine, in which the first change was to the frame, that now had two thick frames inside the wheels. The inside cylinders were replaced by outside cylinders, situated between the plates. The crank axle bearings were on the inside frames and the carrying axles on the outside frames. These became standard for Crewe from their introduction up to 1857, either built as 2-2-2s or 2-4-0s. Buddicom was later replaced by Francis Trevithick, son of the locomotive pioneer, who remained in charge at Crewe after it became part of the London & North Western (L&NWR) in 1846. He went on to develop the Crewe standard. By the 1850s, he had introduced a 2-2-2 with 7ft drive wheels and a distinctive castellated chimney.

John Gray was another engineer who was to add to the variety of designs available in the 1830s. He took out a patent for a new arrangement for a 2-2-2, in which the leading and trailing axles were mounted on an outside plate frame, while the crank axle was fitted to boxes on the inside frame. The first engines to use his design were built for Hull & Selby in 1840 by Shepherd and Todd of Leeds. At the time of the patent, he was a mechanical assistant on the Liverpool & Manchester, but from 1840 to 1846, he was locomotive superintendent for the Hull & Selby, where he designed engines with far higher boiler pressures than were usual at the time: The norm was 70psi, but he raised that to 100psi. His design was taken up by David Joy of E.B. Wilson & Co. with a 2-2-2 for the London, Brighton & South Coast that was named *Jenny Lind* after the popular soprano. The name stuck, and the class became known as Jennies.

Robert Stephenson made one major change to the Patentees in the 1840s with the introduction of the Long Boiler locomotives, patented in 1842. He had carried out initial experiments on the North Midland and the result was a locomotive in which to compensate for the better steaming and longer boiler tubes, the firebox had to be moved to a position behind the rear axle. The engine had outside cylinders and was notably wobbly when in use. In order to combat that problem, the wheel arrangement was changed to a 4-2-0 with the cylinders moved to a position between the leading wheels.

In 1845, the Gauge Commission was set up to try to solve the problems caused where the Stephenson and broad gauge met. Brunel suggested a trial between locomotives working on the different lines, each running on equivalent lengths and gradients of track. Stephenson chose a Long Boiler engine to take part in the trials carried to compete with a GWR Firefly class. The Stephenson engine was a new variation, with the driving axle just in front of the firebox and the cylinders towards the centre of the boiler. In the trial it was described as 'unsteady', but Stephenson put that down to an uneven track. Using the same engine, he carried out a demonstration run between Darlington and York, achieving speeds of between 50 and 60mph. In the end, the trial was meaningless. If one performed better than the other, was that due to the gauge or the quality and performance of the rival locomotives? In any case, there was never any question of converting the 4ft 8½in gauge to 7ft, with all that would be involved in changing all the infrastructure from moving platforms further apart at stations to widening bridges and tunnels. On the other hand, it was a simple matter to add a third rail between the two broad gauge rails to allow the tracks to be used by trains on what would now be the standard gauge. The writing was very much on the wall for the broad gauge, which was a major disincentive to develop locomotives for that system.

One development of the Long Boiler was the work of Thomas Russell Crampton, who had worked for the GWR and patented his idea in 1843. It was known that speed could be increased by having larger driving wheels. There was a general belief, however, that locomotives needed a low centre of gravity for stability, which limited the height to which the axle of the drive wheels could be set. Crampton's answer was to place the drive wheels behind the boiler, which could then be kept low down. The only problem was that there was less weight bearing down on the driving wheels, thus giving less traction. However, the long boiler and the extra steam it provided compensated. As a result, Cramptons were built with 8ft diameter drive wheels. Crampton set up

in business on his own. His first two engines went to Belgium for the Namur-Liege line, but in 1848 he built *Liverpool* for the L&NWR, that was later recorded at a speed of 62mph with a 180-ton load. When one considers that in 1829 many considered the idea of a locomotive being able to manage a 20 ton load and reach a speed of 10mph, it is a measure of just how far things had come in less than two decades. There is, however, one element of the locomotive that has not yet been discussed which was, in its own way, just as important as any other type pf development: valve gear. It is somewhat complex, and is the subject of the next chapter.

CHAPTER TWO

Valves and Valve Gear

The *Handbook for Railway Steam Locomotive Enginemen*, published by the British Transport Commission in 1957 neatly summed up what a valve is required to do:

When the regulator valve is opened, steam generated in the boiler passes through the internal steam pipe, through the external steam pipe to the steam chest, where the supply of steam to the cylinders is regulated by the action of the valves. In the cylinders the steam expands and does useful work on the piston before escaping into the atmosphere.

The job of the valve gear is to ensure that the different events take place in the correct order and with the correct timing. The valve gear also has another function; it can be used to put an engine into reverse.

From very early on, locomotives were fitted with slide valves, which consisted of a static base, with openings to allow steam into and out of the cylinder, and the movable portion which, as the name suggests, slid over the openings, shutting or opening them. At first, this was a comparatively simple affair, with steam being admitted through most of the time the piston was moving, before being shut off, after which the exhaust port would be uncovered. In time, this operation became more sophisticated, with the introduction of 'lap' and 'lead'. Lap is the amount by which the valve overlaps the steam port at dead centre – steam lap on the live steam side and exhaust lap on the exhaust side. Lead is the amount by which the steam port is open when at dead centre. The diagram below shows a typical slide valve.

The valve, working with the valve gear, ensures that a precise series of events occurs in the cylinder. It begins with admission of live steam up to a cut-off point, followed by a period when the steam expands in the cylinder. This is followed by the exhaust of the used steam, then by a period of compression when the valve is closed. There is then a brief period of pre-admission of live steam, before the piston starts the next working stroke. Exhaust lap is generally used for slow, but heavy duty work, such as shunting, when the maximum force is supplied by the expanding steam. Again, this is easier to understand by reference to the following diagram that shows the

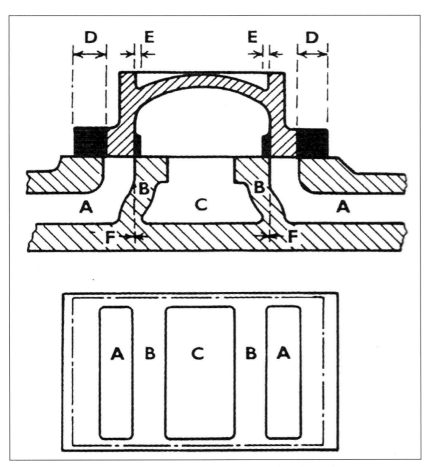

Plan and elevation of a slide valve, in which A are the two steam ports, B the bridge and C the exhaust port, D the steam lap, E the exhaust lap, F the exhaust clearance and G the lead.

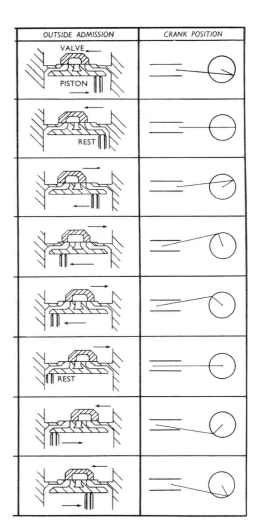

OUTSIDE ADMISSION	CRANK POSITION

The valve events of a slide valve for one revolution of the wheel

movement of the valve relating to the position of the crank for one revolution of the wheel.

A locomotive needs to be able to move both forwards and in reverse. The drive from the piston is taken via a system of connecting rods to the crank, either connecting to a pin on the crank on the wheel for an outside cylinder engine or to the cranked axle of an inside cylinder. With a crank, the rods push the crank pins under the axle and pull them forwards over it in forward gear, and push over and pull under in reverse. To achieve this change in direction requires an appropriate mechanism, the valve gear. In the case of *Locomotion,* the locomotive was fitted with slip eccentric gear. A stop collar is fitted to the drive axle and drives the eccentrics by means of a small drive pin. A slot in the stop collar allows the eccentrics to slip, that is move freely, for part of the rotation of the wheel, before the pin engages and starts to move the slide valve. This was the device used for reversing *Locomotion* but it needed to be manually operated. This involved unclipping the operating rod and reattaching it when the eccentric was correctly positioned for reverse movement. As a result, the driver, instead of standing on a conventional footplate, had a position on a footboard alongside the boiler. By the time *Rocket* was being designed, the system had become rather more sophisticated. Various devices were in use, mostly with fixed eccentrics activated by gabs, V, X or Y shaped, that could engage with different pins to change direction. On *Rocket,* the gabs were operated by a foot pedal.

A different system was developed for the Planet class. The valve actuating rods were moved to the front of the cylinders, though the treadle was retained to move the eccentrics sideways for forward or backward movement.

The slide valves were moved by two long rods attached to the cross rods ahead of the cylinder. The rods were attached to two curved levers on the footplate that oscillated while the train was in motion. Seeing the replica *Planet* in action at its home at the Science and Industry Museum in Manchester makes one realise how unusual this arrangement was; one is simply not used to seeing two long levers constantly in motion on a footplate.

One major advance was made in 1834 by a Liverpool engineer, James Forrester. He used two eccentrics on the drive axle, one for forwards and one for reverse. There were two gab hooks, in between which was a pin attached to the valve spindle. To move forward, the upper gab was lowered onto the pin. To reverse, the upper gab was lifted out of the way and the lower gab engaged. It was both simple and effective. There were other variations, but all had something in common, a fixed cut off point for admitting steam into the cylinder. To use a modern analogy, it was rather like having a motor car with just one forward and one reverse gear. It would work, but it would hardly be called efficient. One of the first to remedy this situation was John Gray who patented his 'horse leg' valve gear as part of the patent of 1838 mentioned in the previous chapter. He first applied it to a Liverpool & Manchester Railway locomotive *Cyclops* in 1839. The he moved to the Hull & Selby, where several locomotives were fitted with the new gear. It differed from earlier gears in that the change between forward and reverse was no longer abrupt, but smoothly continuous. The gear was, however, complex and hard to move, so that it needed a double reversing handle to make it work – rather in the way a 'waiter's friend' corkscrew is jointed, to provide maximum leverage to get the cork started and then shifts for the easier part of finally removing it. What the patent makes quite clear is that Gray fully realised that the continuous movement was more than just another way of getting an engine to change direction. It could also be used to alter the way in which the steam was used in the cylinder. It would make for more efficient working, but other engineers were slow to take up the idea. Perhaps it was the difficulty of working the mechanism that deterred them. The next very important advance came not thanks to an established engineer, but from an apprentice.

William Williams was a 'gentleman apprentice' at the Stephenson works in Newcastle, which means that his parents paid for him to be taught draughtsmanship and be given practical instruction, without having to go through the stages of working his way up from menial tasks. He was investigating a complex X-type gab gear, which was difficult to work, with different pins which, if not properly seated, caused damage. He devised a slotted link, with the forward gear eccentric coupled to the top of the link and the reverse to the bottom. The links could be raised or lowered by a reverse rod operated from the footplate. As with the Gray valve gear, this ensured continuous, smooth operation. He worked on developing the idea with one of the company's pattern makers, William Howe.

A model of the new arrangement was sent to Robert Stephenson in August 1842, who at once saw its value– 'On first blush it is very satisfactory' – and he declared that if it worked in practice, the inventor should be suitably rewarded. But who was the inventor? Both Williams and Howe claimed the honour, and the dispute has never really been satisfactorily settled. As with so many such cases, the truth is that both probably made significant contributions, but the original idea was certainly Williams'. Neither, however, has given his name to what was to be simply known as the Stephenson gear, because it was first used at the Newcastle works. The gear was first fitted to a 2-4-0 in 1842 and immediately proved its value. The detailed working is best explained with reference to the following diagram.

With the new gear in place, the driver now had two methods of controlling the power of the engine. He could use the regulator to open the valve in the dome to allow more or less steam into the cylinders and he could also use the reverser to change the cut-off point at which steam was admitted to the cylinders. When starting the engine, full power is needed to overcome the inertia, and again when faced with a steep slope, much as one has to start a car in low gear and change down for hills. The reverser will be full forward, with the cut-off point as late as possible, allowing the maximum amount of steam into the cylinder. The steam will still be under considerable pressure as it is exhausted, hence the loud chuff-chuff as an engine gets under way. As the engine gathers speed, the reverser can be moved back, with a much earlier cut off, allowing the steam to expand in the cylinder. Variable cut off allowed for far more economical working, much to the delight of railway operators. Not surprisingly, other engineers soon began to use the Stephenson linkage or produce variations of their own to avoid the Stephenson patent.

Daniel Gooch devised a system that he claimed was an entirely new invention, and therefore no royalties were due to Stephenson. In the latter system, the valve spindle is fixed, and the reversing rod moves the expansion link

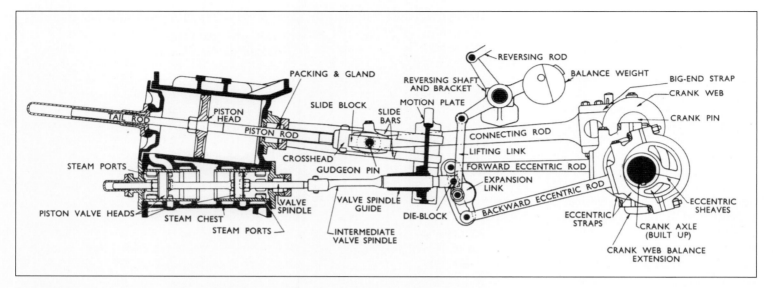

The Stephenson valve gear as illustrated in the British Transport Commission Handbook for Steam Locomotive Enginemen. In this case the diagram shows a piston valve instead of a slide valve, but the mechanism is the same.

and the forward and backwards eccentric rods. In Gooch's version this was reversed: the expansion link was attached to a fixed bearing and the reversing rod moved the valve rod. Its use was virtually limited to the GWR. At Crewe, Alexander Allan came up with yet another variation, in which the reversing lever moved the eccentric rods, the link and the valve rod. Neither of these received as wide a use as the Stephenson linkage, but a serious competitor did appear, not from Britain but from Belgium.

Unlike in Britain, the Belgian railway system was developed by the state. The first section was opened between Brussels and Mechelen, a point half way on the line to Antwerp, in 1835 by Belgian State Railways. The arrival of the railway excited one 15-year-old living in Mechelen, Egide Walschaerts. He was a keen modeller, and when he displayed his work at a local exhibition, he was encouraged to study engineering at the University of Liège. He joined the railway workshops at Mechelen, rapidly rising through the ranks until he was appointed works superintendent, a position he was to hold for the rest of his career. It was here in 1844 that he designed his valve gear, which was patented but for some reason under the name

Walschaert, without the final 's' and this version is still occasionally found although with the 's' is more common.

Here there is just a single eccentric, attached to the eccentric rod, which in turn is attached to the expansion link that allows for both reversing and varying the cut-off point. A second system, based on a radius rod attached to both the piston cross-head and the valve spindle, ensures that the lead on the valve remains the same in both directions, regardless of the cut-off point. This represents an improvement over the Stephenson system where, when the cut off was less than a quarter way through

the stroke, the excessive lead allowed steam into the piston. The following diagram should help to make the arrangement more easily understood. It took some time for the Walschaerts gear to be accepted in Britain, and the Stephenson gear remained in general use and dominated British locomotives up to the end of the nineteenth century. The slide valve also remained in use throughout the period covered in this book. The only other type was a piston valve that was developed by W.M. Smith of the North Eastern Railway but was never widely used. Piston valves only came into general use in the 1920s.

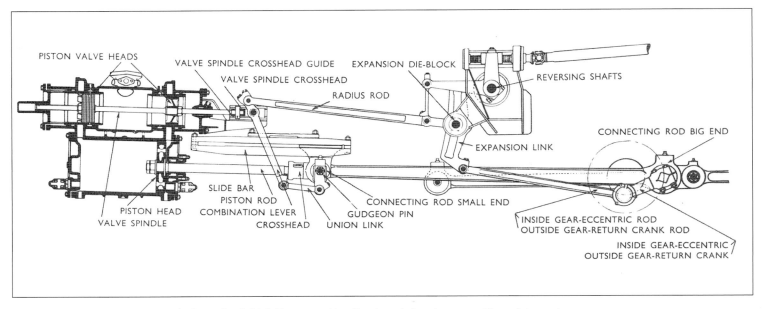

The Walschaerts valve gear, again from the British Transport Handbook and showing use with a piston valve.

CHAPTER THREE

A Rich Mixture

The great diversity that existed in railway locomotives and rolling stock by the middle of the nineteenth century can be seen from the catalogue for the Great Exhibition mounted at the Crystal Palace in 1851. It lists some 200 railway exhibits, including several locomotives. The first locomotive that visitors saw was *Lord of the Isles*, the last of the GWR's Iron Duke class built at Swindon that year. It stood outside and was an imposing sight, with its 8ft driving wheels. A curious feature was the seat on the tender for a 'travelling porter', who perched on high, was there to pass messages between the footplate crew and the guard. Among the other imposing locomotives were several already mentioned here, including, Trevithick's *Cornwall* and Crampton's *Liverpool.* The latter was given special attention as the most powerful engine on show, rated at 1,140hp, just surpassing the GWR single at 1,000hp.

There was also a selection of five locomotives representing what was, in effect, a new type of locomotive: the tank engine, where the boiler water is stored in a tank attached to the boiler rather than in the tender. There were three main types in use: side tanks, in which the two tanks either side of the boiler reached down to the running plate; pannier tanks, which were similar, except that the tanks left a gap above the running plate; and saddle tanks, which as the name suggest were wrapped over the top of the boiler. A few well tanks with the tank below the boiler were also brought into use. These had been developed for specialist use, usually where short runs or heavy duty were required. Strictly speaking, the first tank engine was *Novelty* at the Rainhill trials, but that was not a line of development that was followed through. Forresters produced two 2-2-0T engines for the London & Greenwich in 1836-7, but again there were no immediate successors. The new generation of tank engines began to appear in the mid-1840s. A typical example is the *Great Britain* a 0-6-2T built by McConnell of Bromsgrove for the Midland Railway in 1845. It was specifically built as a banking engine to help the regular locomotives haul trains up the Lickey incline on the main line between Birmingham and Gloucester, which at 1 in 37.5 was too steep for locomotives to manage unaided. McConnell had earlier imported two American 4-2-0s to do the same job and converted them by adding saddle tanks Another early version built by George

England in 1848 was for the contractors working on the London, Brighton & South Coast Seaford branch. A Kitson, Thomson & Hewitson 2-2-2T intended for goods traffic was among the medal winners at the Exhibition.

One area of continual development not mentioned so far was the gradual change from coke to coal as a fuel. Coke was more expensive than coal and had only been used because of the Liverpool & Manchester Act which had specified that an engine had to 'consume its own smoke'. Attempts to use a mixture of coke and coal began early, with experiments on *Patentee* and *Star*. At the same time, Edward Bury provided a locomotive, *Liver*, to the Liverpool & Manchester. This had a Chanter type firebox, patented in 1834. It was divided horizontally into two compartments, the upper grate fed with coke, the lower with coal in the ration 75 per cent coal to 25 per cent coke. The grates were constructed of water tubes. When one of the grate tubes broke in 1837, it injured both driver and fireman. The engine was temporarily withdrawn and the firebox rebuilt with a vertical instead of a horizontal divider.

From the 1840s onwards, there were several fireboxes designed with air inlets in the sides. One of the most successful was the work of D.K. Clark who built them for three lines, the North London, the Eastern Counties and the Great North of Scotland. The latter used steam jets for the inlets and continued with them on all their locomotives from 1860 to 1880. Several variations on divided fireboxes for the two fuels continued right up to the end of the 1850s, with varied degrees of success. Attempts to use just coal were hampered, largely because the fireboxes were never big enough to allow a free passage of air through the fire. This was not so much of a problem when coke was

the fuel. It was developments on the Midland that finally brought a satisfactory solution, after experiments that began in 1856 and ran for the next four years. The answer was the setting of a brick arch across the front of the large firebox, to deflect the flames over a longer path. This was often combined with a deflector plate above the fire door to deflect extra air over the fire, an arrangement that lasted throughout the age of steam.

So far, we have only been looking at two main gauges, the broad Brunel gauge and the standard Stephenson gauge, but narrower gauges were being built, mainly for very short lines serving specific industries. Zerah Colburn's *Locomotive Engineering* of 1864 lists a number of these, including 2ft 6in gauge at Willenhall Furnaces, a mile long 2ft gauge near Wigan that had a 1 in 50 grade and was being worked by a geared locomotive in 1861 and a 0-4-0 built for the Neath Abbey ironworks which was exhibited at the International Exhibition of 1862. The Crewe works had its own 18in gauge, worked by a 2½ ton locomotive appropriately named *Tiny*. These were short, private lines and made little impact on the wider world of railway development. The same could not be said of the railway that is generally thought of as starting the real age of narrow-gauge railways, the Festiniog, later given the Welsh spelling Ffestiniog.

The line was constructed in order to bring slate from the mines and quarries of Blaenau Ffestiniog to a new port being developed, now known as Porthmadog. This involved building a causeway, the cob, across the Glaslyn estuary. The cob was completed in 1811 but the Festiniog Railway Company was only formed twenty years later. The 2ft gauge line rose 700ft in 12 miles with an average gradient of 1 in 92. It was originally worked by horses, and the slate came down under gravity for most of the journey, and the horses were only required to go up the hill with empty trucks. The original engineer was James Spooner, but it was his son Charles who decided to take the line into the steam age. The first locomotives were ordered from George England of the Hatcham Ironworks of New Cross, London. The first four delivered in 1863 were all 0-4-0 saddle tanks, but because of their small size also had a tender, so officially designated as 0-4-0STTs. Three of these remain on the line and represent a record for continuous use of steam locomotives for over a century and a half. Another original was the *Little Giant,* unofficially known as 'the boxer' because the piston movement was like a series of short arm jabs, that sent it swaying from side to side. According to Spooner's own account, 'a speed of 8 or 9 miles an hour is the greatest at which it is possible to run without incurring the risk of breaking the springs or loosening the driver's teeth'.

Although originally intended purely for freight, the line received a Board of Trade certificate for passenger carrying, and proved very popular, as indeed it still is. There was a problem, however, in providing locomotives with sufficient power to take on the extra loads. It was not possible simply to increase the size of the engines because of the very sharp curves on sections of the track. The solution was found by Robert Fairlie. The engines he designed look like two locomotives that have backed into each other and got stuck together. There are two boilers, with a central cab in between. Each boiler is carried on a separate four-wheel bogie creating an 0-4-4-0T configuration. This meant that, on the curves, one bogie could be pointing at an angle to the other. The locomotives were built in 1879, again by George England. The Fairlies were successful but in time it was realised that more conventional locomotives were equally capable of working the line. The success of the Festiniog proved that narrow gauge railways were a practical proposition for mixed traffic. One of the first new lines to adopt a narrow gauge was the Isle of Man's 3ft gauge line that linked Douglas to Peel and Ramsey. It opened in 1873 and now operates between Douglas and Port Erin. Early locomotives were supplied by Beyer Peacock and Number 4, a 2-4-0T, is still in use on the line as is an 0-6-0T by Dübs & Co. of 1885.

Many more narrow-gauge lines opened up throughout the latter part of the nineteenth century, some purely industrial lines, some serving mines and quarries also providing passenger services and some simply aimed at the tourist trade, such as the Lynton & Barnstaple, that took a wavering course between the two towns. But the most important area of development was in Ireland, where narrow gauge lines played a vital role in providing links to rural areas. By the end of the nineteenth century, twenty companies were operating with an immense variety of locomotives from different manufacturers. Among the most remarkable engines to be seen on any narrow-gauge line were the 5 Class built for the County Donegal Railways Joint Commission by Nasmyth, Wilson & Co. at the start of the twentieth century. The extensive 3ft gauge line was spared the elaborate curves that were such a feature of so many narrow-gauge routes, and as a result were able to use far larger and more powerful locomotives, and these 2-6-4T engines are outstanding examples.

Another new type of steam railway was introduced in the 1860s. The Metropolitan Railway was authorised by parliament in 1854, but work only got under way in 1860. It was the first underground railway to be built in a city and was designed to link the main line stations of Paddington, King's Cross and Euston, used increasingly by commuters, to Farringdon in the City of London. Unlike the later tube service, it was built by means of digging a deep cutting and then covering it over. Surprisingly, it was agreed to build it to take broad gauge trains from Paddington, though a third rail was later added. The first locomotives were designed by Daniel Gooch, 2-4-0s with 6ft diameter driving wheels. Relations between the GWR and the new company were far from harmonious and when the former threatened to withdraw their locomotives and rolling stock, the Metropolitan simply ordered standard gauge locomotives and stock from the Great Northern (GNR) as a temporary measure until they had locomotives of their own.

There had already been one other locomotive designed for the broad gauge by Sir John Fowler and built at the Stephenson works in 1861 that was known as 'Fowler's Ghost'. It was unique in that it was described as 'fireless'. In fact, there was a small furnace that was used to heat firebricks to white heat that were then stowed in a space in the boiler barrel, where they provided enough heat to raise steam for short journeys. The idea was that the furnace could be used in a conventional manner when running in the open, and the firebricks in the tunnel. It was not a success. Fowler then reverted to a more conventional design, with a series of 4-4-0T locomotives that were to remain more or less standard until the line was electrified. They were designed to use smokeless fuel, coke originally

and later Welsh steam coal. A unique feature was that the steam had to be condensed, rather than simply being allowed to blow out into the confined space of a tunnel. A first batch of eighteen were built in 1864 by Beyer Peacock and as the line expanded so the demand for engines grew. Eventually, around 120 were built, the last of the class only being withdrawn in 1948.

Returning to more conventional railways, the second half of the nineteenth century was marked by the proliferation of companies large and small spreading throughout the whole of Britain, many of which had their own engineering works, with their own mechanical engineers, each of whom had his own design ideas. There were also manufacturers supplying locomotives as required, sometimes to their own design and sometimes meeting the requirements laid down by their clients. The result is an almost bewildering array of styles, shapes and sizes. There is, however, one unifying factor; all were to some extent, looking for greater power, whether to pull heavier loads or to attain greater speeds or, in many cases, to do both. We shall be looking at some of the key developments of the period.

Competition between the different companies was a factor, especially when they were offering alternative routes from one part of the country to the other. The classic example is the choice between travelling from London to Scotland by the east coast route, either starting out with the GNR from King's Cross to Edinburgh or taking the London and North Western from Euston to Aberdeen. The rivalry culminated in what became known as the 'Races to the North'. A series of fast runs were made in July and August 1888, but with lighter trains that those that would have normally been in use. Both averaged over 50mph, the slightly better time being on the west coast line that covered the 392½miles to Edinburgh in 6 hours 27 minutes. Nothing had been settled and in August 1895 there was another race, this time to Aberdeen. The prize went to the west coast route again and the two companies, L&NWR and Caledonian, where the 540 miles were covered in 8 hours 32 minutes at an average speed of 63.3mph Once again, there was very little difference, with the GNR taking just 6 minutes longer. These times were partly due to improvements in the track, but the races were also a demonstration of the even greater improvements that had been made in express locomotives in recent decades. Two of the locomotives that took part in the races have been preserved and are now in the National Railway Museum at York, and they both show most of the major improvements that had been made over the years.

Patrick Stirling, the son of a Kilmarnock clergyman, became locomotive superintendent for the GNR and designed what became known simply as the Stirling Single, the first of which was built at Doncaster in 1870. Its name derives from the size of the driving wheels at 8ft 1in. With a 4-2-2 wheel arrangement, the Singles are arguably the most elegant locomotives built in the Victorian era, full of sweeping curves over the driving wheels and outside cylinders and a dashing livery of green, with red, yellow and black lining. Two of these engines took part in the classic 1895 run, No. 668 completed the run from King's Cross to Grantham at just over 60mph and No. 775 continued to York at a sparkling 65½mph.

Francis William Webb was, coincidentally, also the son of a clergyman, the rector of Tixall. He served his apprenticeship at Crewe under Francis Trevithick and became locomotive superintendent in 1870. He designed what became known as the Precedent Class of 2-4-0 locomotives, one of the last of which was *Hardwicke* built in 1892. The driving wheels were smaller than those of the Stirlings at 6ft 9in, but there were two pairs of driving wheels, and it was worked at a pressure of 150psi, slightly lower than that of the Stirling. The locomotive has none of the glamour of the Single but proved itself a powerful engine and never more so than on the run from Euston to Aberdeen on 22 August 1895. *Hardwicke* had the toughest part of the west coast route, from Crewe to Carlisle that included the climb over Shap Fell and still managed the fastest run of any of the locomotives that took part, with an average speed of 67.2mph, such an extraordinary feat for the time that the driver on the day, Ben Robinson, deserves a mention. There seems to be no record of the name of what must have been his very hard-working fireman. Altogether, 166 locomotives in this class were built between 1874 and 1894 and proved not only fast and powerful, but durable: *Hardwicke* remained in service until 1932, having covered nearly a million and a half miles, while others in the class are said to have kept going for two and a half million.

These two locomotives have been selected for special treatment for several reasons. They were outstandingly successful, they both took part in the famous races, they are still preserved and they represent the two main trends in locomotive design in the last half of the centuries – coupled driving wheels and singles. One of the more extravagant singles was designed by J. Pearson and built for the Bristol & Exeter broad gauge at the Rothwell Works in 1853. This was the 4-2-4T express tank engine *Rothwell*, with two four-wheeled bogies and a massive pair of 9ft diameter driving wheels. By contrast, the London area was dominated in the early years by 4-4-0T engines. The first were delivered from the Stephenson works for the North London in 1855, followed by six Hawthorn Cramptons for the South Eastern in 1857. But by far the most successful were Beyer-Fowler tanks that were built for the Metropolitan and District lines. Altogether, 120 were built and did most of the work right through until the lines were electrified in the early twentieth century. Other companies used the reverse of the 4-4-0T – the 0-4-4T, where in most cases the water was in a back tank situated over the trailing wheels. One of the most successful of all the tank engines of this period was the London, Brighton & South Coast A1 Class, popularly known as Terriers, so called because the sound of the exhaust was said to be like that of a barking dog. Designed by William Stroudley, these 0-6-0 side tank engines first steamed out of the Brighton works in 1872 and fifty of them were produced over the next eight years. Although weighing in at a modest 24 tons, they were noted for fast acceleration and running speed, which made them ideal for handling the commuter traffic in the south London area, with its many stations and short runs in between. They were taken up by other companies and often, when retired from the LB&SCR, they found new homes on other lines, which explains why a total of ten of these busy little engines have been preserved. Equally successful were the Great Eastern Railway (GER) 0-6-0T engines that worked out of Liverpool Street from 1890. Hard workers, they had to cope with 15 stops in the 11-mile run to Enfield. Even larger tank engines had come

into service, the biggest being the 4-4-2Ts built for the London, Tilbury & Southend to a design by William Adams. They were outside cylinder engines and the first 4-4-2T with cylinders between the frames only appeared for the first time on the Taff Vale in 1880.

Throughout the second half of the nineteenth century, progress in developing freight locomotives was slow and unenterprising compared with the progress that had been made with passenger expresses. Typical locomotives were 0-6-0s. The trains clanked their way along with loose-coupled trucks and although continuous braking had been compulsory for passenger trains from 1889, the rules did not apply to freight. As truck carrying capacity only rose from around 6 to 20 tons per wagon, there was little incentive for change. It was only at the end of the century in the 1890s that Francis Webb introduced more powerful 0-8-0s onto the L&NWR.

One of the more obvious changes to locomotive appearance in the second half of the century was the boiler cladding. Early locomotives looked fine with polished wood on the outside, but water could seep through the planking, reducing its effectiveness. An outer iron casing solved the problem and the timber disappeared from view. Less obvious were the various methods used to balance the moving parts. At first, this was limited to the wheels, and the most successful early experiment was made by John Gray for his 0-6-0s on the Hull & Selby. He added weights to the wheel rim opposite the crank arm, an idea that was gradually taken up by other engineers. By the 1850s, balancing had been applied to reciprocating as well as rotating parts. One other major change was the replacement of slide valves by piston valves, though it was not until 1888 when W.H. Smith developed his version that they very gradually came into general use. A much less obvious change but one of considerable importance was the greater use of steel in place of iron for both locomotives and track. Bessemer furnaces, introduced in the late 1850s, enabled steel production to be hugely increased and consequently brought down the price.

Another technical development of the period was concerned with making more efficient use of the steam raised in the boiler. Compounding had been used on stationary engines since the end of the eighteenth century. It had been recognised that exhaust steam was still under pressure after it had left the cylinder, so instead of being allowed to simply escape into the atmosphere it was fed into a second cylinder. The low-pressure cylinder was larger to compensate for the lower pressure and ensure even running. Francis Webb designed the appropriately named *Experiment* for the L&NWR in 1882. It was a 2-2-2 fitted with three cylinders. The two high pressure cylinders were 11½in diameter, and fed into a 26in low pressure cylinder. Unusually, the two pairs of driving wheels were not coupled, but driven independently. Altogether, twenty-nine engines of this type were built. He later went on in 1899 to produce a more powerful Teutonic class, with 7ft 1in diameter driving wheels and working at the high boiler pressure of 175psi.

Towards the end of the century, another engineer began to make a name for himself. Henry Alfred Ivatt was born in 1851 and joined the GNR as an apprentice at the age of seventeen. He later moved on as locomotive engineer for the Great Southern & Western Railway of Ireland, where he gained a reputation for designing very successful 4-2-2 locomotives with side fireboxes. He returned to England to take up the post of chief mechanical engineer at the GNR. He is best known for introducing Atlantic 4-4-2 locomotives to the GNR in 1898. He was also the first to use the Walschaerts gear in Britain. His one patent was, however, nothing to do with locomotives, but for a new method of opening sprung carriage windows. Anyone who has travelled in a vintage carriage will be familiar with the device with its stout leather strap. This was a new age of large engines, and one of the grandest was designed by David Jones for the Highland Railway, the first 4-6-0. These were tough engines for a difficult terrain with sharp curves and gradients as steep as 1 in 60. The three pairs of coupled driving wheels were flangeless to help the large engine negotiate the curves.

Rail safety was greatly improved by the arrival of more efficient braking systems. As mentioned earlier, Stephenson had introduced steam brakes, but these were later largely abandoned in favour of air brakes. The first examples were simple, with pressure being applied from a main air reservoir by means of a valve on the locomotive. The pressure was transmitted to the brakes through pipes to the carriages on the train. There was a problem, however, that the effect was not instantaneous throughout the whole train, so that vehicles nearest to the engine braked before those at the far end. This problem was overcome by an American engineer, George Westinghouse. He set up the Westinghouse Air Brake Company in 1869 and in 1872 he introduced his automatic air brake, which had a triple valve, so called because it allows air into the reservoir, applies pressure on the brakes and releases them. In his system, there were separate air cylinders under each vehicle in the train, allowing for continuous braking. The following year he introduced the vacuum brake system. The Westinghouse air brakes were first used in Britain by L&NWR in 1872.

In 1875, the Midland began a series of trials on different braking systems that eventually came up with a resounding victory for the Westinghouse air brake, which was soon adopted by many other companies, the system now being manufactured from a new works at King's Cross.

The last decade of the century saw the construction of two mountain railways in Britain, the most ambitious of which was a rack railway to the summit of Snowdon. It was not Britain's first rack railway – the pioneering Middleton Colliery Railway had used the system right back in 1812, in order to get extra traction from a light locomotive, after heavy engines had broken track on other lines. But the idea had not needed to be developed, once track had improved. Not surprisingly, mountain railways had already been developed in Switzerland, and the locomotives were supplied by the Swiss Locomotive and Machine Works, based on a design already in use on the Brienz Rothorn Railway. The track used the Abt system, with the toothed rack set centrally between the rails. The locomotives were built with sloping boilers so that, on the steepest sections, the water level remained constant. On this line, the locomotive is always behind the train, and steam power is used for the ascent. On the descent, where gravity does the hard work, the locomotive is kept in forward gear while running backwards, in effect acting as a brake, with air instead of steam puffing out from the cylinders. All the 0-4-2T engines on the Snowdon line were built by the Swiss company. The only comparable mountain railway is the Snaefell on the Isle of Man, opened in 1895, but is in effect a continuation of the Manx electric tramway and was worked with normal adhesion traction, with no need for a rack system

The second half of the nineteenth century had seen a whole range of improvements in design, producing ever better performances but with little or no attempt at standardisation across the whole spectrum of the country's railway. There were, however, new forms of transport and new forms of motive power to challenge the railways. Up to now, the steam railway had been by far the quickest and most efficient way of moving around the country. But in Germany, two engineers, Karl Benz and Gottlieb Daimler, were developing internal combustion engines to power motor cars and motorcycles, offering individuals the choice of travelling wherever they liked whenever they liked, regardless of timetables. And in Brighton, the Volk Electric Railway started operations in 1883, providing a clean, efficient power source, albeit one still in its infancy. At the start of the twentieth century, railway engineers continued their search for more power and speed.

CHAPTER FOUR

The Edwardians

The Edwardian period takes us into the twentieth century, but in terms of railway development it is an artificial distinction. There is no abrupt change of direction, merely a continuation of the process of development. One important new area of improvement concerned the fundamental force itself – steam power. When steam comes from the boiler it is 'saturated', which is to say that it is on the cusp between liquid and vapour. It will contain minute water droplets, which will condense out as the steam expands as it does in the cylinders. Once water begins to condense out, then more is formed, using the original droplets as nuclei. The effect is to reduce the effective force of the steam in moving the piston. The hot water is passed through, which has used up energy, but which provides no useful work. The answer was the development of superheating, in effect reheating the steam in its passage between boiler and cylinder. There were early experiments in the nineteenth century, in which steam drums were placed in the smoke box, but were not very effective. The answer was found not in Britain, but in Germany, where Wilhelm Schmidt produced a very effective superheater for the Prussian

State Railway around 1900. It was brought to Britain in 1906 and became widely used.

The Schmidt superheater consists of U-shaped tubes, the elements, through which the steam passes, held inside boiler tubes, the flues, through which hot gases pass. The effectiveness depends on the number of elements, but also how hard the engine is working. The good news was that the harder the engine worked, the more efficient the superheating became. There was a problem, however, in that when using saturated steam, the water droplets were quite efficient lubricants. Using superheated steam inevitably meant that valves in particular were worn down more quickly. This was especially true of slide valves and led directly to the increased use of piston valves.

One area of notable improvement was the development of more powerful goods locomotives. Ivatt designed the K1 class (later renamed Q1 class) 0-8-0 locomotives that first went into service in 1901, popularly known as 'Long Toms'. Previous locomotives had found difficulty coping with trains of fifty coal wagons, partly because of a lack of suitable sidings to accommodate them. But with sidings made larger and shunting engines more powerful, the new locomotives were able to take trains of sixty wagons on the run from Peterborough to London. The boiler was adapted from one originally used for 4-4-2 engines, cylinders were 19¾in diameter and slide valves were used. Over the next decade, cylinder size was increased to 20in., superheaters were added, and the slide vales replaced by piston valves.

It was not just the goods trains that required extra power. Improvements in passenger coaches made them heavier. The first sleeping cars had been introduced on the North Eastern in 1894 and a much improved 12-wheeled sleeper in 1900. Luxury Pullman coaches had appeared on the Midland in the 1870s offering dining facilities, and general dining cars for all passengers were introduced on the GNR. The introduction of corridor carriages meant that passengers could actually use a toilet on board, and in 1900 the Flying Scotsman, the name given to trains on that route in general and not just the well-known preserved engine, was able to offer a service with dining cars and corridor coaches with toilets from King's Cross to Edinburgh, without having to take a 20 minute stop at York, rather euphemistically known as a 'lunch break'.

Among the most successful designs to emerge at the beginning of the twentieth century were the GER 'Claud Hamiltons', so called because the first of the class was named after the then chairman of the company. Designed by James Holden and Frederick Vernon Russell, they were very distinctive, with brass capped chimneys, curved splashers, a square firebox and a polished steel smokebox surround. With a 4-4-0 wheel arrangement they more than matched the various ten wheeled locomotives that were beginning to appear. The original still had slide valves on the inside cylinders and were fitted with the Stephenson motion. They were able to haul trains of up to 400 tons at an average speed of 49mph on the 130 mile run from Liverpool Street to North Walsham, even though there were ruling gradients of 1 in 70 and 1 in 95. One very different feature was a good example of turning a problem in one part of the works into a solution in another. The company had its own gas works to provide gas for carriage and station lighting. They were fined for discharging the oily waste product into the River Lea, so they decided to use the oil to fire the engines. Steam-powered injectors were used to spray atomised oil into the firebed. The class was modified over the years but remained the leading express locomotive for the company until steam power came to an end.

Ivatt designed the first of the big boiler locomotives, with boilers of 5ft 6in diameter, designed for free steaming on main line expresses. The first of these 4-4-2 Atlantics took to the rails in 1902 and was originally fitted with side valves. A number of variations appeared. In 1904, Ivatt's first compound was introduced with the high-pressure cylinders outside the frame driving the rear coupled wheels, and the low-pressure inside working on the other front pair. A special valve arrangement meant that the engine could either be worked as a compound or with the cylinders working separately. A slightly different arrangement was used on No. 1300 built at the Vulcan foundry for Ivatt. The cylinder arrangement was the same, but this time the valves allowed it to be worked as a two-cylinder engine when starting, but was automatically switched to compound working as it gathered speed. Later changes included changing to piston valves and adding superheating.

Atlantics became popular with many companies, but it is interesting to see that on the east coast route to Aberdeen the different companies involved had very different ideas about the detail – and very different end results. The GNR engines suffered from often rather crude construction that led to some rough rides. Where the GNR had gone for wide fireboxes, the North Eastern had narrow, round-topped fireboxes but the construction was of a very high quality and the Z class were notable for their silky-smooth running. The North British had Belpaire fireboxes, large outside cylinders with piston vales but wretchedly poor suspension and as a result gave by the worst ride of the three. It is not unreasonable to say that the differences were often the result of arbitrary decisions by individual engineers and certainly not down to any scientific approach to reaching maximum efficiency.

One company that had to make what was in effect a new start in locomotive design was the GWR. Once they had lost the gauge war, development of broad-gauge engines more or less came to an end and the last broad-gauge train had run in 1892. The man in charge of the transition was William Dean, who had become chief engineer in 1877 and retired in 1902. He was responsible for the design of the City Class shortly before his retirement, but the actual job of completing the work was left to his successor, George Jackson Churchward. The 4-6-0s were the first to have the tapered boiler that was to be a feature of GWR express locomotives. The boiler had a greater diameter at the firebox end than at the smokebox, which was said to have the advantage of having a larger volume of water close to the fire. It had another advantage in that when coming over the brow of a hill, there was a tendency for water in the boiler to run towards the front of the engine, risking uncovering the crown of the firebox. With the tapered boiler this does not happen. The most famous locomotive of the class is *City of Truro* that achieved fame as the first locomotive ever to claim reaching a speed of 100mph on 9 May 1904 hauling the Ocean Mail from Plymouth to Bristol, the record being broken when a speed of 102mph was recorded when going down Wellington bank. The word 'claim' is used deliberately, for there is considerable scepticism about whether any accurate speed measure was made. If that was indeed the speed reached, then it was a record that was not broken until 1935.

Churchward was unusual among engineers in being open to ideas from other parts of the world and in carrying out a series of experiments to find long term solutions to the problems likely to be faced by traffic increases and heavier loads in the future. The City Class was followed by the first series of his experimental locomotives, the Saints, two-cylinder engines, originally built as 4-6-0s though later versions were 4-4-2s. His next venture was to move towards four-cylinder engines, and the company brought over three four-cylinder 4-4-2 compounds from France. In the meantime, he prepared his own four-cylinder engine that was also built as a 4-4-2 but simple not compound and was designed so that it could easily be converted into a 4-6-0. It used ideas borrowed from the French, including the arrangement of the cylinders. The inside cylinders were placed under the smokebox and drove the front set of driving wheels and the outside cylinders were in line with the rear bogie and drove the other set of driving wheels. He found some difficulty in fitting everything into the available space, which led him to abandon the Stephenson linkage he had previously used for an adapted version of Walschaerts'. The prototype was named *North Star*, and the whole class became known as Stars. He was constantly looking for improvements. The Stars were followed by Knights that had the new Swindon Number One superheaters. A third series was inaugurated in 1909 as 4-6-0s. They were the first King class locomotives, but are not to be confused with the later powerful King Class of the 1920s – these first Kings were renamed at that time. No. 4021 *King Edward* was very appropriately selected to haul the funeral train of Edward VII in 1910. In time there would be more amendments and improvements – the Kings were followed by the Queens, with improved superheaters, then the Princes with enlarged cylinders and in 1914, the Princesses appeared with a new and better braking system to cope with longer and heavier trains. One other Churchward locomotive deserves a special mention. *Great Bear* was built in 1908 as the line's first Pacific, a 4-6-2, with four cylinders, an enormous boiler and wide firebox and at 71ft it was one of the longest engines of the day.

The outbreak of war in 1914 marked a turning point in railway history. The government took over the running of the whole system and development came to a virtual standstill, only really to begin again in the 1920s. So, this is a good time to look back over the century that had passed since the world's first commercial railway began operations at Middleton Colliery in 1812. The first decades had concentrated on colliery engines, trundling at gentle pace heaving coal from the mines to navigable

rivers and canals. Everything changed with the opening of the Liverpool & Manchester, the first line to carry both goods and passengers on steam trains, and the first to have a locomotive with an efficient way of raising and using steam. Since then, every element of the locomotive was developed and improved to create ever more efficient and powerful machines. If one remembers that at the Rainhill Trials of 1829 the requirement was to build a locomotive that could travel a level track with a train of 20 tons at 10 miles an hour and that the maximum allowable weight of the locomotive was 6 tons and then compare that with the performance of *City of Truro,* the advance is remarkable. Whether the latter really did pass the magic hundred figure, it certainly came close to it – and instead of 6 tons the locomotive weighed 95 tons and was hauling a train of around 150 tons. And the importance of railways in this period cannot be overestimated. They opened up travel for all and were by far the fastest mode of transport on the planet. Britain had led the way in the railway revolution, and development had been in the hands of a great many engineers working for a whole variety of different companies. This in turn led to a huge variety of different styles and methods of working that all go to help make this period so fascinating. It was to be the last time for steam to have a virtual monopoly on the railways. The steam trains on the underground section of the Metropolitan were never popular with passengers and in the 1890s the first electric trains began to run and the electrification of the whole tube network got under way in the early twentieth century. Electrification of other lines would follow. It would not be long after the end of the First

World War that the first diesel engines and diesel railcars would appear. Yet even so, by the middle of the twentieth century there were still over 200 different classes of steam locomotive running in Britain. But it was during the first century that the greatest changes occurred, and the richest variety was to be found.

The aim of this introduction has been to give an overall picture of the main lines of development, with appropriate manufacturers and types used to illustrate the different trends. Inevitably, in such a short space many companies and interesting engines have had to be omitted. Some of these omissions will be made good in the following pages. The illustrations have been arranged geographically by individual companies rather than chronologically. This is intended to give a clearer picture of the ways in which different companies designed their engines rather than attempting just to show a pattern of historical development, though that too will emerge. Although the title of the book refers only to Victorian and Edwardian locomotives, it seemed logical to extend the period up to 1914 and the start of the Great War, which effectively marked a temporary end to locomotive development for the country's railways.

In the following photo section, readers might notice that light railways have not been completed. They have been treated as a separate category and appear in the companion volume covering the rest of the British Isles.

PHOTO SECTION

Southern England and Channel Islands

The Jersey Eastern Railway was a standard gauge railway opened in 1873 and ran along the south coast of Jersey from St Helier (Snow Hill) to Gorey Pier in the east of the island. One of the Kitson constructed 0-4-2 tank locomotives *Calvados* is seen at the head of a train at Gorey station c1905. The Jersey Eastern Railway closed in 1929 with all rolling stock subsequently scrapped.

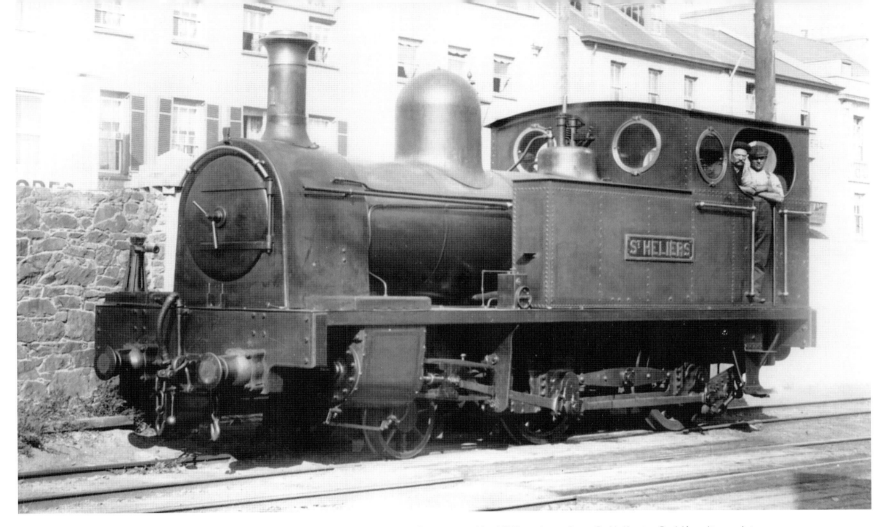

The Jersey Railway started life as a standard gauge railway which first opened in 1870 and ran from St Helier to Corbière. It was later converted to 3ft 6in gauge, with the first re-gauged services operating from 1885. No. 1 *St Helier* was a Manning Wardle 2-4-0 tank dating from 1884. The railway struggled financially from the beginning, finally succumbing to poor passenger numbers in October 1936.

The Isle of Wight Railway was opened in 1864 and operated from Ryde Pier Head to Ventnor, with a branch to Bembridge. The company had a fleet of standard Beyer Peacock constructed 2-4-0 tanks, of which locomotive No. 4 is here seen on a passenger service in the 1890s. The Isle of Wight Railway became part of the Southern Railway at the railway grouping in 1923.

The Isle of Wight Central Railway had an eclectic fleet of mostly second-hand locomotives. However, in 1906 the company acquired a then in vogue self-propelled Hawthorne Leslie steam rail motor, which served until 1918 when the locomotive portion was separated from the carriage portion. The separated locomotive portion was then employed as a shunter, with the passenger section being used as an ordinary bogie carriage. The Company ran a number of services on the island, including the former Cowes and Newport line, a main line from Newport to Ryde St Johns Road and branches to Sandown and Ventnor West.

The Freshwater, Yarmouth and Newport Railway, served West Wight and was opened in 1888, with the line connecting the towns in its title and serving a notably rural and thinly populated part of the island. Locomotives Nos. 1 and 2 are seen at Newport shed. The Company had to rapidly acquire the locomotives along with some second-hand Manchester Sheffield and Lincolnshire Railway four-wheeler carriages when it fell out with the Isle of Wight Central Railway in 1913. The latter company had originally operated all traffic since the line opened for goods traffic in September 1888 and to passengers in July 1889. Both locomotives were purchased second-hand, with No. 1 an ex-Pauling & Co contractors Manning Wardle 0-6-0 tank constructed in 1902, formally named *Northolt*. No. 2 was a former LB&SC, A1 Terrier No. 46 *Newington*, which along with a sister locomotive had been first sold to the L&SWR in 1903 for use on the Lyme Regis branch.

The Cowes & Newport Railway was the first on the Isle of Wight to open in June 1862, with two 2-2-2 well tank locomotives being constructed by Slaughter Grüning in 1861 and named appropriately *Precursor* and *Pioneer*. *Pioneer* is captured by the photographer c1885. The line was later taken over by the Isle of Wight Central Railway with the original pair of locomotives, both withdrawn in 1901.

The London Brighton & South Coast Railway (LB&SCR) under William Stroudley produced some notably handsome locomotives, with a fine example of his artistry being his B1 0-4-2 passenger class. No. 176 *Pevensey* was constructed at Brighton Works in 1890. These beautiful locomotives were very striking in their bright original lined yellow gamboge livery. They hauled some of the most important trains on the Brighton mainline and other principal LB&SCR routes after 1882.The photograph was taken c1895.

Another fine example of William Stroudley's craftsmanship in the form of D1 0-4-2 tank No. 255 *Willingdon*. Introduced in 1873, these sturdy tank locomotives were used on outer suburban trains and were often seen at principal Brighton Company stations, notably Victoria, London Bridge and Brighton itself. First deployed on station pilot work, they were later cascaded to lesser duties on quieter branch duties and for shunting, lasting until early British Railways days in traffic. The final member of the class formally titled *Riddlesdown* was eventually sold to the Whittingham Hospital Railway in Lancashire and was only finally withdrawn in 1958.

By the turn of the twentieth century, the LB&SCR had in service a fine fleet of modern steam locomotives including the elegant H1 'Atlantics' designed by Douglas Earl Marsh. No. 425 is seen in all her resplendent Marsh umber lined livery glory and is about to head south on an express service at Victoria Station. c1912.

The LB&SCR purchased two steam rail motors from Beyer Peacock in 1905 for evaluation trials against two Dick Kerr petrol rail cars. The steam rail motors were deemed not to be worth developing as a type, with the Company opting instead for 'push and pull' motor train hauled by modified A1 and A1X 0-6-0 Terriers tanks for light branch line services. Both LB&SCR steam rail motors were, after first being loaned to the government in the First World War, eventually sold to the Trinidad Railway, where they worked for a decade or more.

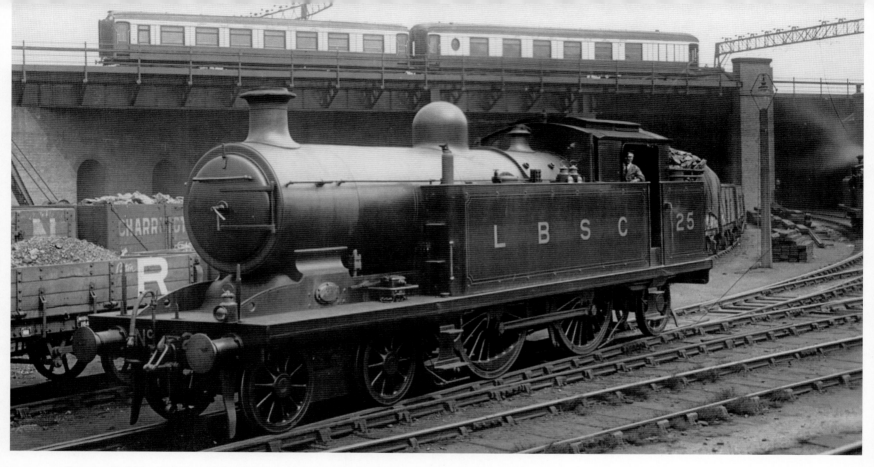

Douglas Earl Marsh designed the 'I' 3 Class 4-4-2 tanks for express passenger work. Introduced in 1907, No. 25 was one of the batch constructed between 1909-1910 and is seen here at Battersea awaiting its next turn of duty. These 'Atlantic' tanks were some of the first locomotives to demonstrate the advantages of superheaters in Britain. Fitted with the German Schmidt version, examples were pitched against George Whale's 'Precursor' class 4-4-0 express tender engines of the mighty L&NWR in a famous trial from Rugby to Brighton. The smaller tank design would consistently demonstrate superior economy in coal and water over the larger Crewe built design. The 'I' 3 class were a significant improvement on the Earle Marshes' notably weak 'I' 1 and 'I' 2 4-4-2 tank classes. A number of 'I' 3 Class locomotives would last into nationalisation in 1948, with the last example withdrawn in May 1952.

The London Chatham & Dover Railway (LC&DR) was something of a church mouse affair, with a very mixed bag of locomotives. This was due to the company's poor financial state, which was partly due to its ongoing fight in Kent for traffic with the rival South Eastern Railway. Continually short of funds, William Martley, the railway's first Locomotive Superintendent, often had to resort to purchasing locomotives from manufacturers that were failed orders. The four *Europa* Class 2-4-0 tender locomotives, were designed by him and were constructed by Sharp Stuart in 1873. *Asia* was one of the four locomotives used on some of the company's most important trains, including the Post Office mail service via Dover for the continent. c1898.

Albion was one of six Large Scotsman Kirtley D Class 0-4-2 Well Tanks constructed by Neilson & Co in 1872 to a design by William Martley for suburban services. They were prone to prime badly, a consequence of their domeless boilers, with water carried over from the boiler to the steam chest and cylinders; a potentially dangerous and destructive situation as water cannot be compressed. This led to an accident at Holborn Viaduct in 1874, when *Albion* collided with a locomotive hauling a string of wagons. The driver had been trying to stop the locomotive from priming and being distracted had run through a signal at red. The class was in service for many years on suburban and branch line services, before being gradually withdrawn at the turn of the twentieth century. The 0-4-2 is pictured at Longhedge, Battersea shed in the mid-1870s. Note the basic weatherboard open style cab and much ornate brass work.

LC&DR Hercules Class as pictured reconstructed as a 0-6-0 saddle tank. One of two 0-6-0 tender goods locomotives named *Hercules* and *Ajax* both constructed by Hawthorn in 1859. They were sold to the LC&DR in 1860, where they worked for some years before eventually being reconstructed as saddle tanks for shunting. They both survived until 1895. No. 143 is seen at Longhedge c1894.

The first two 'Mail Singles' were introduced on the South Eastern Railway in 1861, followed by eight more examples of the class in the early 1860s. They were strong reliable machines and featured on the important tidal mail trains from Folkestone to London until 1885. No. 72 is seen here in its re-boilered condition in the early 1880s, painted in dark green and fully lined out; note the extensive brass trim and fittings of the locomotive. It was constructed in 1865. The class gradually became replaced on express passenger work by new 4-4-0 tender locomotives introduced from the 1870s. No. 72 was finally withdrawn in October 1887.

One of two Neilson crane tanks supplied to the South Eastern Railway in 1876. Both had a long service life, surviving through the South East &Chatham Railway period after 1899 and into Southern Railway ownership after 1923. The last example was withdrawn from Stewarts Lane in July 1949. The twin crane locomotives were normally to be found respectively working at either Brick Layers Arms or at Ashford Works in Kent.

A James Stirling B Class 4-4-0 No. 459 seen here in lined Prussian green livery in 1901. First introduced in 1901, as principal express passenger locomotives for now operationally unified SECR express services, No. 459 was used in experimental oil firing trials in 1901 but was later converted back to coal firing. The majority of the type were reconstructed into B1 class after Harry Wainwright became locomotive superintendent in 1899, however a number retained there domeless Stirling boilers until final withdrawal in 1911.

James Stirling introduced the A Class 4-4-0 passenger locomotives from 1880. These were initially used on important express services between the coast and London on the South Eastern Railway but were later cascaded on to secondary work and branch line duties. No. 36 is depicted in full Wainwright lined SE&CR green. Displaying its Stirling parentage, it features a domeless boiler and distinctive wing plates. Withdrawals commenced in the early 1900s, with the last examples gone by 1908.

One of the most beautiful express steam locomotives ever constructed in Britain was Harry S. Wainwright's D Class 4-4-0 of 1901. This fine example No. 730 is seen at Herne Hill station in 1906 with a train of non-corridor stock. In reconstructed 'D1' form they were fitted after 1921 with a modern Belpaire firebox, Maunsell superheater and with piston valves replacing the original slide valve type. The rebuilds had a decided 'Derby' look to them, the influence of Midland Railway protégé James Clayton who had joined the SE&CR at Ashford Works in 1914 as Chief Draughtsman. An already successful design was thus further improved, with Richard Maunsell producing through his rebuilds of Wainwright's original 4-4-0's a cost effective and useful new fleet of modern two cylinder 4-4-0's. Both types lasted on passenger services for more than fifty years. The final original D was not withdrawn until 1956 from Guildford Shed, with the final reconstructed D1's going in November 1961.

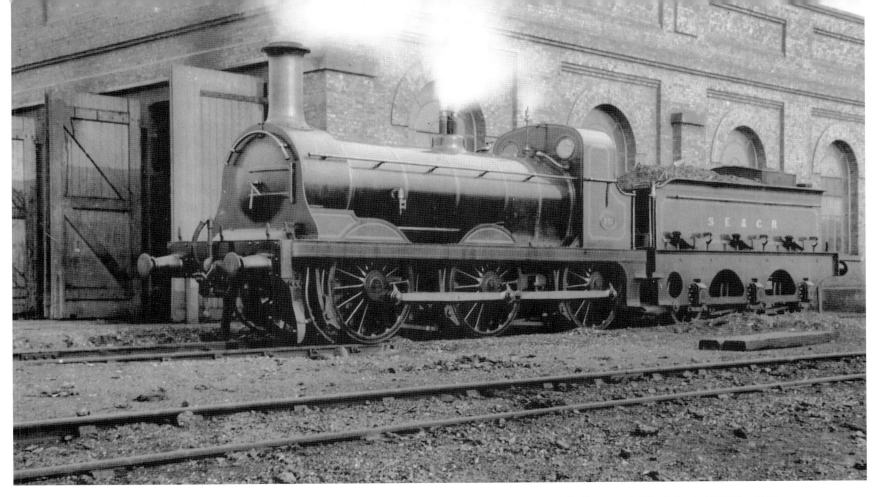

James Stirling O Class 0-6-0 tender goods No. 251 is seen here in elaborate fully lined Wainwright livery at Ashford shed c1905.The O Class was introduced in 1878, a dependable well-crafted design of goods locomotive, able to perform in a multitude of tasks and often seen on goods and passenger trains. A number of examples were sold out of service to the East Kent Railway, near Dover and remained in service long after the last examples on the Southern Railway had been withdrawn. Many were subsequently reconstructed by Wainwright to become O1 class, with the last member of the class not withdrawn until June 1961.

SE&CR Kitson steam rail motor No. 2, here seen at Chatham Central station c1906. These rail motors were first introduced in 1905 and featured a single third class compartment which seated 56 passengers. They were designed for use on lightly used passenger services, though they proved to be a disappointment in traffic. They lacked the required tractive effort to haul an additional unpowered trailer, with only a single four- or six-wheel coach not over taxing them on workings. All were withdrawn by 1919, with the locomotive section scrapped and the carriage portion turned into articulated two car sets for further service on branch line services.

London & South Western Railway (L&SWR), No. 81 *Herod* was a Falcon class 2-4-0 tender locomotive, designed by Joseph Beattie and introduced in 1866. The Falcon class were designed to replace 2-2-2 passenger locomotives also designed by Joseph Beattie. These had been found to be wanting on fast services to Southampton from Waterloo. The new class were more capable, featuring larger coupled wheels and greater tractive effort. They were constructed at the L&SWR then principal works at Nine Elms in south London and lasted in traffic until the last examples were withdrawn in 1898.

Joseph Hamilton Beattie was responsible for designing a large number of 2-4-0 classes, the most famous of which were the Beattie Well tanks originally used for intensive London suburban services. Long lasting, the class was subsequently modernised by both William Adams and Dugald Drummond, with the latter fitting some with new domed boilers and his trademark 'lock-up' style safety valves. A total of six differing 2-4-0 well tanks, with each one featuring small incremental improvements to the overall design, were introduced to assess which was the most suitable. This proved to be the Nelson class of 1858, with No. 143 a fine example of the type constructed at Nine Elms Works in 1858 and withdrawn in 1882. Classed as 0298 under the L&SWR classification scheme, these useful 2-4-0 Well Tanks were used on suburban and branch line duties, with three of the later reconstructed Adams examples dating from 1874 lasting until December 1962 in Cornwall on Wenford Bridge branch duties.

The 330 Class 0-6-0 saddle tanks were a standard Beyer Peacock design supplied to the L&SWR in 1876. Examples were also constructed for the Swedish State Railways, while other variants were exported to Australia for use on government railways. No. 330 was the prototype of the class on the L&SWR. The type was extremely long lived, with examples surviving on the East Kent Railway and the Kent & East Sussex Railway until after the Second World War. No. 330 was finally withdrawn in 1924 by the Southern Railway.

The Vesuvius class were originally introduced by Joseph Beattie in 1869 for main line passenger work. The class was successful and operated in traffic for many years, being improved several times by successive locomotive superintendents. The last examples were finally withdrawn in the 1890s, with the final two lasting until 1899. No. 280 is captured in reconstructed condition in the William Adams era.

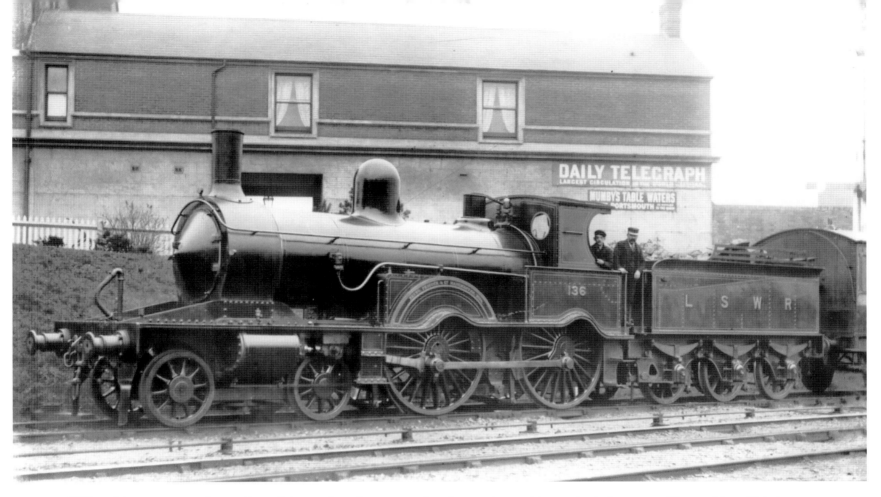

William Adams was a true locomotive artist, one of a unique group of engineers who would go on to design some of the most beautiful steam locomotives of the Victorian era. No.136 was a 135 Class 4-4-0 design, constructed in 1880 for main line express work and is seen after 1898 as adapted by the new L&SWR Locomotive Superintendent Dugald Drummond. No.136 was fitted with an experimental smoke box door in the 1890s. The 135 Class were principally used on important express services to Southampton, Bournemouth and Salisbury, with withdrawals only beginning in the second decade of the twentieth century. The final example of the class was withdrawn in 1924 under a new Southern Railway.

The Adams T6 Class 4-4-0 express passenger locomotives were introduced in 1895, being his last design for the L&SWR before ill health forced him to retire. No. 682 is seen here in original condition shortly after entering traffic, painted in Drummond lined green, but still retaining its Adams stovepipe chimney and other features. The T6 class survived in traffic well into Southern Railway days, with the last not withdrawn until April 1943.

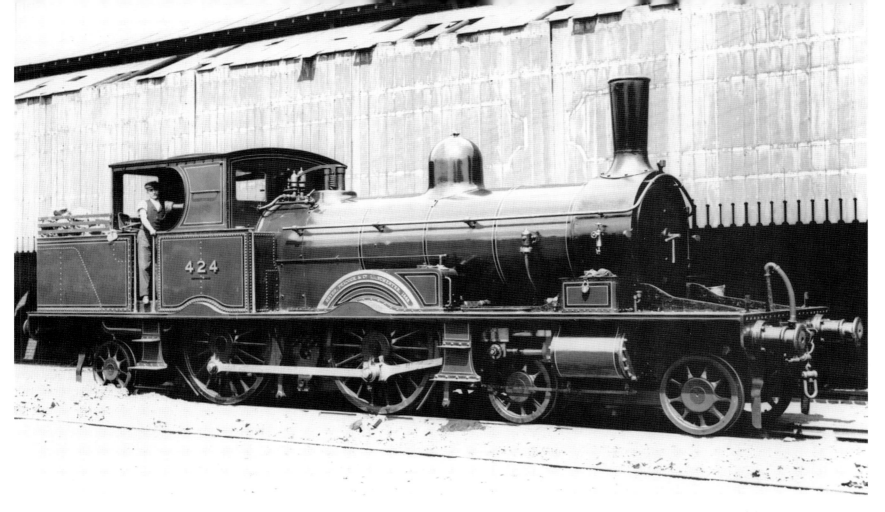

Perhaps one of the most admired tank locomotive designs was the Adams Radial 4-4-2 Tank designed by William Adams for the L&SWR. There were a number of variants from their first introduction in 1882. Members of the class gave good service, being used on suburban services and on some branch lines across the L&SWR system, No. 424 is captured in her original form, with small side tanks and stovepipe chimney. Three examples would last on the Lyme Regis Branch with the last example withdrawn on 29 July 1961.

A Drummond double single 4-2-2-0 No. 373, with two separate sets of drive wheels, heading a train of bogie stock through Clapham Cutting. c1912. These interesting four-cylinder compound locomotives were introduced in 1897 and were not completely successful in service, rather like Francis Webb's earlier three-cylinder compounds for the L&NWR. No. 373 was one of five introduced in 1901 as class E10. These locomotives began to be withdrawn in early Southern Railway days and were all gone by 1927.

The T14 4-6-0 Express locomotives of 1911 were the best of an indifferent crop of 4-6-0 designs by Drummond for the L&SWR. Known as 'Paddleboxes' due to their long valances covering the six driving wheels and these complete with a large glazed 'porthole' on either side for inspection purposes giving them the rakish appearance of an Isle of Wight paddle steamer. The four-cylinder T14s on introduction were viewed as massive engines for the period. As with other larger Drummond designs, they were far from completely successful in everyday service. Another typical Drummond design feature is the large 4,000 gallon 'water cart' double bogie tender, an important requirement for all locomotives running to Bournemouth Central, Exeter Central and Plymouth Friary as the L&SWR lacked water troughs on its principal routes. The class were reconstructed twice, by Robert Urie for the L&SWR and under Richard Maunsell in Southern Railway days. Their distinctive 'paddleboxes' were removed to ease maintenance, while in a final attempt to improve their erratic steaming, Oliver Bulleid fitted them with Urie style stove pipe chimneys. No. 458 is seen with a train of bogie stock running through Clapham Cutting c1913. The last member of the class was not withdrawn until June 1951 under British Railways.

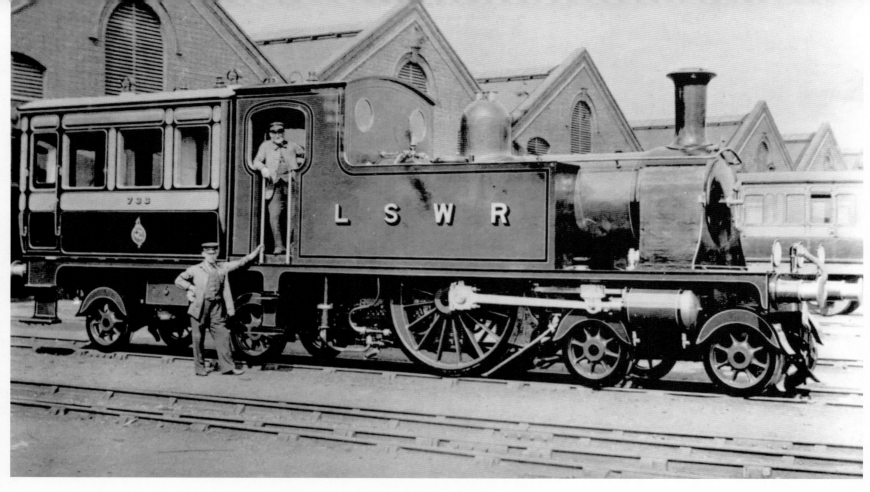

Drummond's famous 'Bug', a 4-2-4 single. This oddity was specially designed by Drummond as an inspection combined locomotive and carriage. Introduced in 1899 and classified as F9 Class, it was used when Drummond went on inspection trips across the L&SWR system, Drummond died in 1912 and his successor Robert Urie did not see the same need for the inspection unit, which after 1912 was rarely seen running. It survived into Southern days however and was put aside to be preserved in a proposed museum at Eastleigh. However, Bulleid had it broken up 1940 as the nation and specifically Lord Beaverbrook called for scrap metal for the war effort. The wooden coach portion has however survived.

Drummond steam rail motor No. 5, constructed in 1905. These were more powerful than the first batch of steam rail motors constructed in 1902, which had proved to be underpowered. The improved H13 units had thirty-two third class seats and were trialled on a wide number of branches across the L&SWR system.

Metropolitan Railway A Class 4-4-0 tank No. 44, constructed in 1869 by Beyer Peacock in Manchester, seen here in new condition, resplendent in its original green livery. These locomotives were the backbone of the services on the first Underground railway in the world, operating in service until electrification in 1905, after which most of them were withdrawn for scrap or in some cases sold out of service for further use by other railways. They were condensing locomotives, with exhaust steam being led from the cylinders through to the two side tanks, an essential requirement for Underground working. By 1936, only one remained in service out of the original forty, No. 23, with this featuring an enclosed cab for working north of Baker Street.

The Metropolitan District Railway had similar Beyer Peacock condensing tanks. No. 14 is seen at New Cross on the East London line c1903, just before electrification in 1905. The District Line locomotives had a different arrangement for the condensing equipment with a large pipe bridging from one water tank to the other and other minor differences to that of the Metropolitan locomotives such as the rear weatherboard for the crews. No. 14 was one of the twenty-four constructed in 1871 for use on the District Railway. Two remained in service after 1905 for engineer's trains, with the last withdrawn in the early 1930s.

The North London Railway began constructing its own locomotives in 1853. Under William Adams, Bow Works produced a series of highly successful 4-4-0 tanks, a type that could be further developed over time, such as an increase in cylinder size from 16in to 17½ in. The NLR also operated services over a number of railways in London, including the LNWR, the GNR and the L&SWR, having only a small mileage of its own. The Company was taken over by the L&NWR in 1909, who had a management and operating agreement with the NLR. John C. Park continued to construct 4-4-0 tanks and introduced his own 0-6-0 tanks for goods work on the line, with the majority of the locomotives constructed at Bow Works. Locomotive No. 67 is seen at Bow Works c1900.

John C Park's distinctive 0-6-0 tank for goods work and dock shunting, of which thirty were constructed at Bow Works from 1880-1905. This picture shows No. 91 at Bow locomotive shed in its distinctive lined NLR blackberry black livery c1912.

The Bow Works Crane Tank, an 0-4-2 tank reconstructed from an 0-4-0 saddle tank supplied by Sharp Stuart of Manchester in 1858 to the North and South Western Junction Railway for services on the short Chiswick branch. In its original form, this small locomotive had worked the Chiswick branch in West London, which ran from South Acton station to a terminus near Stamford Brook, the first railway in the Hammersmith area. The locomotive was later converted to its new use as a crane locomotive and survived until early British Railways days in February 1951, with this remarkable engine then the oldest standard gauge locomotive in the nationalised fleet. The crane tank is seen at the head of the brake down train at Bow Works c1908.

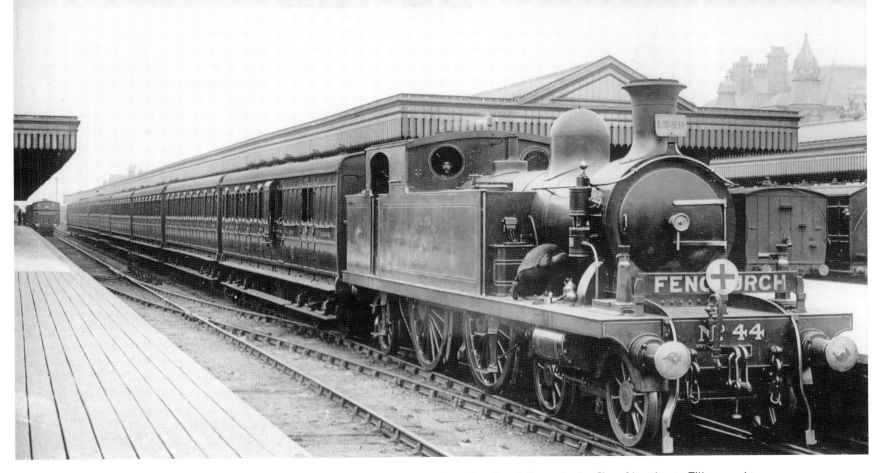

The London Tilbury & Southend Railway (LT&SR) operated a main line from Fenchurch Street in the City of London to Tilbury and to Southend Central Station. The Company had a nepotistic approach to locomotive affairs, employing father and son, Thomas and Robert Harben Whitelegg. Both designed good workmanlike locomotives for the LT&SR, with the passenger types being in the main 4-4-2 tanks. They named them after localities on the line, as did the LB&SCR who followed the practice, this no doubt causing a degree of confusion for passengers catching a train at Fenchurch Street. The Class 37 was designed under Thomas Whitelegg, with No. 44 *Prittlewell* constructed by Dübs of Glasgow in 1898, a year after the class was first introduced. They were the first 4-4-2 tank design to run in this country The locomotive is seen here on a train of the company's smart bogie non-corridor carriages heading for Fenchurch Street.

The LT&SR was absorbed by the Midland Railway in 1912, with the handsome Tilbury tank locomotives losing their distinctive lined green livery for that of the maroon of the Midland. A class 69, No. 71 was a development of the original class 37 introduced under the younger Whitelegg. Originally named *Wakering*, it is seen in 'Midland Lake' on a train of through corridor and lavatory bogie stock to Southend from Ealing Broadway. This popular service was hauled by twin electric District Railway locomotives from Ealing to Barking where steam took over for the final run to Southend Central and the seaside. These distinctive through workings were popular with ordinary Londoners but ended with the outbreak of the Second World War in September 1939.

The 2100 Class 4-6-4 Baltic tank No. 2107 here seen in its Midland livery c1914. Eight examples of large Baltic tanks, designed by Robert Whitelegg, were on order from Beyer Peacock in Manchester when the LT&SR became part of the Midland in 1912. They proved to be something of a white elephant, rather too large for duties over the mainly commuter route, while the GER immediately banned them from running into their terminus at Fenchurch Street due to their 94 ton weight. The Midland Railway followed a 'small engine' policy under CME Henry Fowler and found the mighty Baltic tanks too large for their requirements, though they would also soon feature on the heavy coal trains from Leicestershire to Cricklewood in London during the Great War and were often also seen double heading with smaller Midland Railway locomotives on these important wartime workings. In early LMS days, they were also trialled on semi-fast suburban services from St Pancras to St Albans with mixed results. As a class they were found to be heavy on coal, sluggish performers despite them being fitted with superheaters, though only in combination with 160psi boilers, with the final example withdrawn as early as 1934. Robert Whitelegg would leave the LT&SR's Plaistow Works for the Glasgow and South Western Railway's Kilmarnock Works were he would also design an equally short lived giant Baltic tank design for the Scottish company.

There was once an extensive and complicated railway system criss-crossing the whole of the London docks, with some even featuring passenger operations. No. 7 of the Royal Albert Dock Company stands at the head of a train of GER carriages with a train for Custom House. To help overcome objections to the use of steam traction, some of the locomotives used in the docks were fitted with condensers to help reduce the amount of smoke and steam expelled to the atmosphere from engine chimneys. These engines had a convoluted history in that they were originally constructed in 1849 as L&NWR 2-4-0 tender locomotives at the L&NWR Northern Division's Crewe Works under the direction of the Chief Foreman Alexander Allen. One of three, they were No. 238 *President*, No. 250 *John of Gaunt* and No. 431 *Hercules*. Later reconstructed into a tank locomotive, the engine was sold out of service to the Royal Albert Dock Company and re-numbered as No. 1819, No. 1917 and No. 1911. Connecting with the other London dock systems, the Company even ran 'Boat Specials' for passengers arriving in the Pool of London on Cunard-White Star, Orient Line and P&O liners.

The Millwall Extension Railway operated a passenger service from Millwall Junction on the GER to North Greenwich on the bank of the Thames. Opened in 1871, the railway survived until the General Strike in 1926, when the passenger service ceased to operate. One of the small attractive Manning Wardle 2-4-0 tanks No. 6 is seen hauling a train of four wheeled former GER carriages c1904. Note the Westinghouse brake pump, essential for working with GER carriage stock and the spark arrestor on the long chimney.

GER single 2-2-2 D27 No. 1006 was designed by James Holden in 1885 and constructed at Stratford Works. It is standing on the London Liverpool Street turntable c1900. The advent of effective steam sanding would see a brief revival of 'single' locomotives on principle passenger duties, most notably on the Great Central Railway (GCR), GNR, GWR and Midland Railway. The locomotive was fitted up to burn oil, the residue of producing coal gas to illuminate GER coaches at the Company's own special plant at Stratford in East London. Originally considered to be stronger on Brentwood Bank than 2-4-0's, the locomotives were later used on lighter trains composed of four- and six-wheeler carriage stock, rather than on the heavier bogie stock then being introduced on crack services to North Walsham, Cromer, Ipswich and Norwich. At the same time James Holden was also introducing larger 4-4-0 passenger locomotives to replace the smaller locomotives on these prestige GER express services.

The GER P43 4-2-2s were the final single type locomotives introduced by James Holden in 1898. They only saw service with the company for twelve years, withdrawals taking place from 1907–10. Some of the class were again fitted for oil burning, with the sticky viscous oil kept warm in the adapted tenders through special steam heated coils. They had an elegant look to them, not unlike their contemporaries on the GWR, William Dean's fine *Achilles* Class 4-2-2 singles, with Holden having previously worked at Swindon as the GWR's Carriage Superintendent.

An example of James Holden's S46 4-4-0 tender locomotives. First locomotives introduced in 1900, they quickly became one of the mainstay classes for fast express work on the GER, being used on the most important passenger trains, including the Harwich boat trains and the fast expresses to Norfolk. Known as 'Claud Hamiltons' and named after the Chairman of the GER, they were later fitted with larger superheated round top firebox boilers. Initially designed by A.J. Hill they were later modified under the direction of Edward Thompson, the Head of Stratford Works when Sir Nigel Gresley was CME and classified as LNER class D16/3. The D16/3's also featured extended smokeboxes. Withdrawals began in 1945, with the final four rebuilt examples withdrawn in early 1960.

The GER Y14 Class 0-6-0 tender goods, later LNER J15, was designed by T.W. Worsdell for both goods and passenger traffic and introduced in 1883. They were a numerous and long-lived class of locomotives, with the final examples constructed in 1913. The simple design made for easy erection and that year set a new world record for erecting a steam engine. No. 930 was assembled in only 9 hours and 45 minutes at Stratford Works. During the First World War examples were loaned to the Railway Operating Division of the British Army for service in Belgium and France. No. 525 is seen at Cambridge locomotive shed on 5 January 1910. Members of the class operated on branch lines in East Anglia and also worked on pick up goods work across the system. Withdrawals began under the LNER in and continued throughout the British Railways period, with the last four examples withdrawn on 16 September 1962.

The GER Class 61 were 0-4-4 tanks designed by William Adams during his short tenure at Stratford Works. Introduced in 1878, the class operated suburban trains in the London area and was also to be seen on rural branch lines. Certain distinctive Adams features already appear, most notably the trademark stove pipe chimney and curved styling of the cab. Theses would again feature on his designs for the L&SWR. No. 178 is captured on a Chingford service hauling high density four wheeled carriage stock at an unknown suburban station on the GER c1900.

A Neilson 0-4-0 'Oggy' tank No. 230 at Stratford Works while performing shunting duties c1905. These useful small tank locomotives were to be found across the GER and were mostly used for light shunting in yards and docks, several being based at Stratford Works as works shunters.

The GER had a fleet of small 0-4-0 and 0-6-0 tram engines. These were constructed between 1883-97 at Stratford Works and were used on the Wisbech and Upwell Tramway, as well as for shunting sidings and at dock yards, notably Parkeston Quay, the original name for Harwich. No. 132 is in the process of shunting a train of vans at Yarmouth c1910.

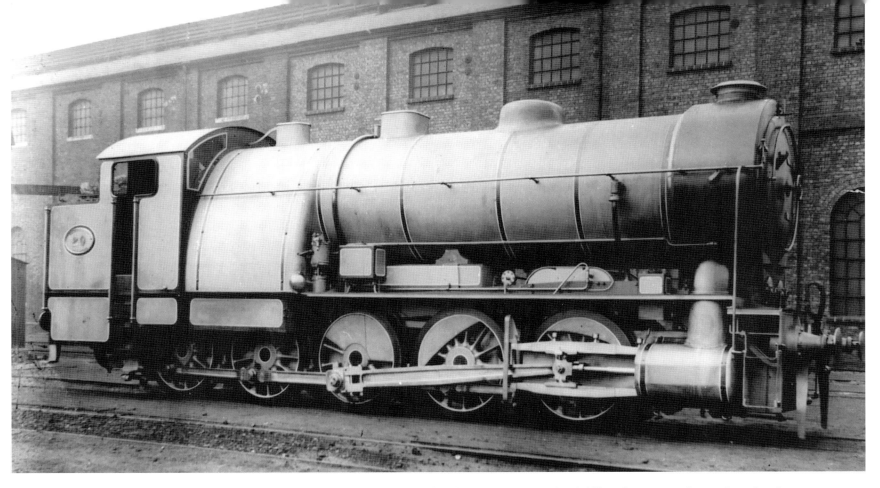

The Decapod was an experimental ten coupled three-cylinder locomotive designed to assess the viability of steam traction against electric traction in the form of the new tube railways. It was the most powerful locomotive in Britain when constructed and was the first to feature an American style round top 'Wootten' firebox, a later classic feature of Gresley locomotives. The locomotive could accelerate a 320 ton train from 0 to 30mph in 30 seconds up Bethnal Green Bank on the steep 1 in 70 climb out of Liverpool Street Station. Designed by James Holden, the locomotive was constructed at Stratford Works in 1902 as GER Class A55. No. 20 was a three-cylinder one off and after extensive trials was withdrawn and reconstructed into a 0-8-0 tender locomotive in 1906, being allocated to Harwich.

The Grand Junction Railway 2-2-2 one of the first locomotives to be constructed at a new Crewe works in 1845. Designed by Alexander Allen. The 2-2-2 tender locomotive was a direct development of the work of William Barber Buddicombe, with the previous locomotive superintendent of the Grand Junction based at Edge Hill and the Company's Chief Engineer Joseph Locke. Known as the famous 'Crewe' type though largely based on designs originally developed at Edge Hill; an express passenger locomotive, hauling some of the most important trains on the Grand Junction and later the L&NWR. A product of the Northern Division of the L&NWR, the robust design was multiple light framed Edmund Bury 2-2-0 types used on the London and Birmingham and Liverpool and Manchester railways. The twin cylinders were placed outside, inclined, and supported within their own separate sub-frame; a robust arrangement which prevented the normal thrust of the pistons, oscillation of the valve gear, as well as the coupling rod connected to the central axle, from damaging the main frames. Clearly the arrangement worked well; with the type proving long lived, while being capable of further development, with Benjamin Connor on the Caledonian Railway introducing the type to Scotland, while later David Jones for the Highland Railway would base both his celebrated 4-4-0 and 4-6-0 designs around the L&NWR original. This example features a later Webb domed boiler, chimney and cab and was based at Northampton. A reminder of earlier Northern Division days under John Ramsbottom was the retention of a slanted smoke box door, with this featuring a separate top fixed section and an opening bottom door.

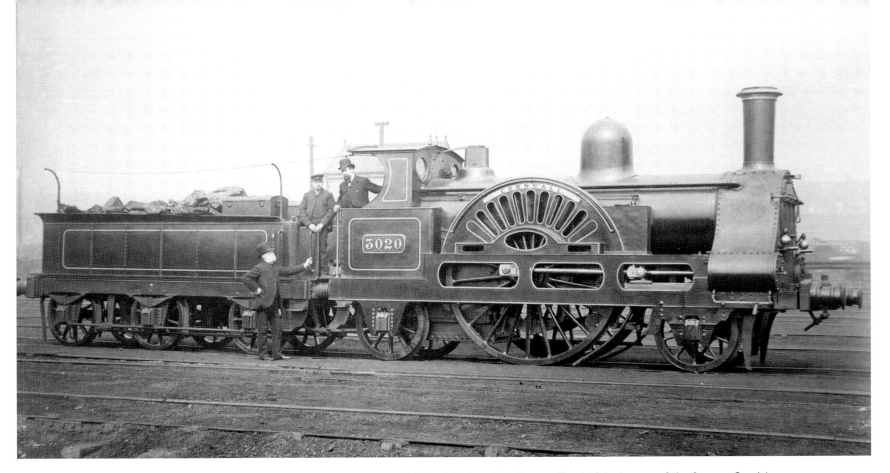

Cornwall was a unique 2-2-2 tender locomotive constructed in 1847 and designed by Frances Trevithick, the son of the famous Cornishman and pioneer Richard Trevithick, in collaboration with Thomas Crampton, as an experimental locomotive. Originally the 2-2-2 had a low slung boiler to fit between the frames, with its enormous single 8ft 6in wheels towering over the rest of the locomotive. Fears that a high centre of gravity could end in derailments would haunt designers of the period, notably Crampton whose low slung designs were intended to eliminate such a possibility, while also providing a long, ample boiler. Robert Stephenson, with his 'Long Boiler' designs, was also battling with the same centre of gravity problem. *Cornwall* was later reconstructed in more conventional form, giving many years' service hauling inspection saloons and occasional ordinary passenger trains on the L&NWR. It was also set aside for posterity by the L&NWR.

Dwarf was a 2-2-2 Well Tank designed and constructed by George England & Co at their works in the Old Kent Road in New Cross London. The Company would later be associated with the construction of single and double Fairlie locomotives for the Ffestiniog Railway in North Wales. Known as the 'Little England' class, a number of them were constructed for the L&NWR to haul ballast trains for the Company's Engineering Department, with one example also being supplied to the Sandy & Potton Railway in Bedfordshire. With an ungainly appearance, the 2-2-2 featured a low slung boiler, fluted dome cover, a raised 'haycock' firebox and notably tall chimney! The little engine never carried a number. *Dwarf* was taken into L&NWR stock when the line was amalgamated into Euston's expanding empire as part of the route of the future 'Varsity Line', the Oxford to Cambridge route.

The L&NWR DX 0-6-0 tender goods was the first locomotive design in Britain to be mass produced, with eventually over 943 being constructed between 1858 and 1874. Some were delivered as saddle tanks, while fifty-four carried names. Eight hundred and fifty-seven examples were constructed by the L&NWR to John Ramsbottom's original Northern Division design of 1858, with a further 86 examples of the original design delivered to the Lancashire and Yorkshire Railway between 1871 and 1874. The DX Class holds the record as the most prolific class of locomotive constructed in Great Britain for a domestic standard gauge railway in the nineteenth century, with DX No.613, the 1,000th locomotive to be constructed by Crewe Works. After 1881, Francis Webb would fit 150psi boilers, with the first examples withdrawn in 1902, a process that was only completed under the LMS in 1930. After 1904, examples were even sold for further work in Holland and Belgium.

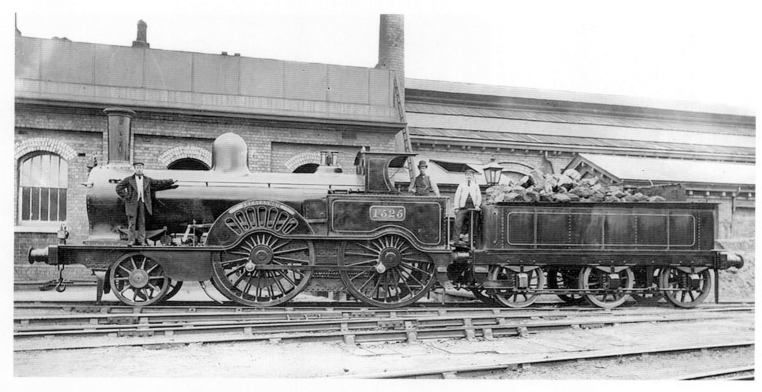

Abercrombie No. 1525 was a Newton Class 2-4-0 tender locomotive designed by John Ramsbottom in 1866. The class was extremely successful, a breakthrough design after Ramsbottom assumed full responsibility for all L&NWR locomotive affairs at Crewe after the dismissal of James McConnel at Wolverton Works by Sir Richard Moon and the subsequent amalgamation of the Northern and Southern Divisions of the Company. Frances Webb would renew the class in the 1880s with new enclosed cabs, standard Webb Crewe boiler and cab fittings, and with their original open splashers filled in; a set of distinctive visual alterations which would signal the arrival of the Webb era at Crewe. In 1873 ten examples were constructed at Crewe for the Lancashire and Yorkshire Railway. Original members of the class would last on secondary duties and engineer's inspection trains, with Webb replacing them with his own 'Precedent' class 2-4-0's. The final example of the original Newton class was scrapped in January 1894.

In 1863, John Ramsbottom introduced a class of 0-4-0 Saddle tank for general shunting, with construction of this simple and distinctive class continued under Frances Webb No,2526 is an example of one of Webb later batches constructed at Crewe Works in 1892.

Under Locomotive Superintendent Frances Webb the L&NWR would introduce eleven differing compound classes, with these developed over time in both three- and four-cylinder forms, featuring high and low pressure cylinders. Webb would seek to further the economic working of the L&NWR by introducing compound passenger and goods tender and tank designs. Controversial to this day, some Webb compound designs seemed to be more successful than others, though it must be noted that the compounds would not last long on principal L&NWR services after his retirement from Crewe in 1903. An example of the Greater Britain class of 2-2-2-2 tender locomotives, No. 3435 *Queen Empress* is captured in workshop grey at Crewe Works after complexion in May 1893. The locomotives were used on important express services and mail trains from London Euston to the North West and to Carlisle on the Anglo-Scotch expresses. The Greater Britain class were again not a complete success in service, only surviving for just over a decade until final withdrawal in 1906.

Along with a number of main line railways in the London area, the L&NWR operated services over parts of the Underground, with through passenger services for a time from Broad Street Station to Mansion House on the Metropolitan District Railway; a so-called 'Outer Circle' service. At first, the company acquired a small fleet of Beyer Peacock 4-4-0 condensing tanks, similar to those of the Metropolitan and the District Railways; however, by the early 1890s the L&NWR replaced these with new Frances Webb 2-4-2 tanks fitted with condensers. The Beyer Peacock tanks were then dispersed to other duties, with some being scrapped in 1892-1893. One was converted into a prototype compound 4-2-2-0 tank, with the remaining examples converted to 4-4-2 non condensing tanks and sent to work in the Manchester area on suburban services from London Road. The class were completely withdrawn by 1907. No. 3080 is seen on a suburban service c1901.

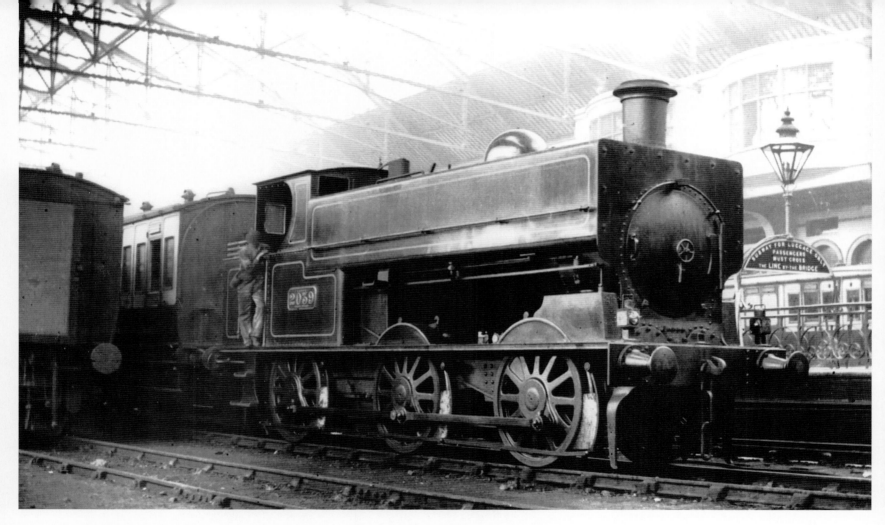

A Webb box tank 0-6-0 No. 2039 at Birmingham New Street Station in 1906 on pilot duties. The tank engine is in fully lined condition, with an overall cab. These useful 0-6-0 box tanks were to be found at various locations operating as pilot and light shunting locomotives and most of these locomotives survived into LMS era, being painted in plain unlined black livery.

Charles Bowen Cooke developed a number of modern classes of locomotive for the L&NWR, among them the inside two cylinder George V Class 4-4-0 tender locomotives of 1910. These locomotives were similar to George Whale's Precursor Class 4-4-0 tender locomotives, but were equipped with superheating. They were used on all important express and mail trains across the L&NWR system. Absorbed into the LMS, weak, thin cracked frames, the Achilles' heel of Crewe Works designs, would signal their departure under William Stanier, with the last example withdrawn under a new British Railways, London Midland Region on 8 May 1948.

George Whale's Precursor class 4-4-0 tender locomotives were introduced in 1904 to replace the Webb compounds. 'Simple' in every meaning of the word, these featured two inside cylinders and recalled the rugged simplicity of Webb's earlier Newton class, but scaled up for modern needs on the West Coast Main line. Their rapid introduction to replace the idiosyncratic but at times capable Webb compound designs, gave L&NWR footplate crews a degree of certainty and reliability which had been absent at times under the autocratic Francis Webb. In 1906, an attractive and capable 4-4-2 tank version was introduced and No. 612 is seen in its original ornate lined black livery in ex-works condition shortly after construction at Crewe Works. The tank engine version was used on outer suburban and some cross-country passenger services across the L&NWR system. Withdrawals commenced in December 1931 with the arrival of new modern Fowler and later Stanier 2-6-2 tank and 2-6-4 tank classes. The final example was withdrawn in February 1940.

An unusual Frances Webb designed 0-4-0 Well Tank introduced for working in dockyards and quays with tight curves, the class were introduced in 1880. The driver and fireman worked at opposite ends, with each being able to couple and uncouple wagons whilst on duty. The 0-4-0s were absorbed into LMS ownership after 1923 when they were withdrawn and scrapped in the late 1920s and early 1930s.

An L&NWR steam railmotor c1905. Nominally designed under George Whale, this self-propelled vehicle combined a small vertical boiler attached to a power bogie, as well as a comfortable carriage divided into two saloons by a central entrance, with one saloon set aside for smokers. Featuring large picture windows for passengers to view the journey, the arrival of competing electric tram cars heavily influenced their interior design, not least in the fitting of tramcar style 'straphangers' and electric lighting powered from batteries topped up by a dynamo. For lighter branch duties, the railmotor was fitted with retractable folding steps for passengers to climb on board from road level, with this proving useful in both North Wales and on the small Hammersmith and Chiswick branch in West London. Though capable of pulling an unpowered trailer, the more conventional arrangement of auto working tank locomotive and trailers proved more flexible, with the final L&NWR example of this distinctive Edwardian self-propelled type, the precursor in many ways of the modern diesel multiple unit. It was withdrawn from Beattock shed in Scotland under a month old British Railways, Scottish Region in February 1948.

L&NWR Claughton four-cylinder 4-6-0 No.1161 *Sir Robert Turnball* in L&NWR 'Blackberry' black c1918-21. With increasingly heavy and luxurious coaching stock constantly taxing existing two-cylinder 4-4-0 and 4-6-0 designs on boat trains to Liverpool, Lime Street and Liverpool Riverside and the famous 'Corridor' to Glasgow Central; Charles Bowen Cooke in 1913 sought to produce a modern four-cylinder design to rival Churchward's Star design, though with mixed results. Undoubtedly, the trial of Churchward 'Star' class against a George Whale Experiment 4-6-0 in August 1910 from Euston to Crewe had got Bowen Cooke thinking. Over reliant on previous Crewe designs rather than developing, as was the case at Swindon, a genuinely new 4-6-0, the engines featured only a 175psi boiler, along with a Schmidt superheater and six 6ft 9in driving wheels. The boiler first fitted was smaller in diameter than Bowen Cook had originally proposed, a product of powerful lobbying from the Engineering Department of the Company who feared the large 77 ton engine would damage their famous 'dustless' prize winning permanent way. The Walschaerts valve gear for the four cylinders was also not set correctly for optimum performance, while the four cylinders were too small and boiler pressure too low at only 175psi on such a large four-cylinder design. In failing to make the successful transition from 4-4-0 to modern 4-6-0, Bowen Cooke was not alone, with both McIntosh of the Caledonian, Manson of the G&SWR and Drummond of the L&SWR all producing similarly underwhelming 4-6-0s before 1914. Under the LMS, the fitting of larger boilers would help improve their performance. No.1161 *Sir Robert Turnball,* named after an esteemed General Manager of the L&NWR, was finally withdrawn in May 1933. The final example of the class was appropriately withdrawn at its birthplace at Crewe on the 23 April 1949.

Archibald Sturrock came to the GNR from the GWR at Swindon in 1850, where he had acted as principal assistant to the great Daniel Gooch. He was responsible for producing a number of significant locomotive designs which in their build and speed had more than a touch of Gooch's advanced broad gauge fleet, but successfully scaled down for a new standard gauge GNR which would reach the capital in 1852. Designed to compete with the best L&NWR express services into the capital from the north, Sturrock would design a notable one off 4-2-2 tender single No. 215 in 1853. Constructed by Hawthorn, the locomotive was an experimental machine and was deployed on express services on the GNR main line, but with mixed results. In service the rigid front end arrangement was less than ideal for an express locomotive, with this eventually replaced by a proper swivelling bogie. The locomotive lasted in service until 1869 when it was then broken up by Doncaster Works.

Patrick Stirling, a famous leading figure of Victorian locomotive design, became Locomotive Superintendent of the GNR after Archibald Sturrock in 1866. Along with Adams, Johnson and Stroudley, he was also an artist, belonging to a distinct group of locomotive superintendents; all of whom would go on to construct engines of genuine beauty and elegance. The famous Stirling 8ft single was probably one of the finest locomotives of the nineteenth century. No. 1006 is here depicted running c1880. As with both Stirling brothers' creations, the engine featured a domeless boiler and trademark polished safety valve bonnet. A very fine example of this school of Victorian elegance, photographers of the period wanted to capture these fine machines, the very latest technology of the time and the noble body of men who drove and fired them, the Concorde pilots of their age.

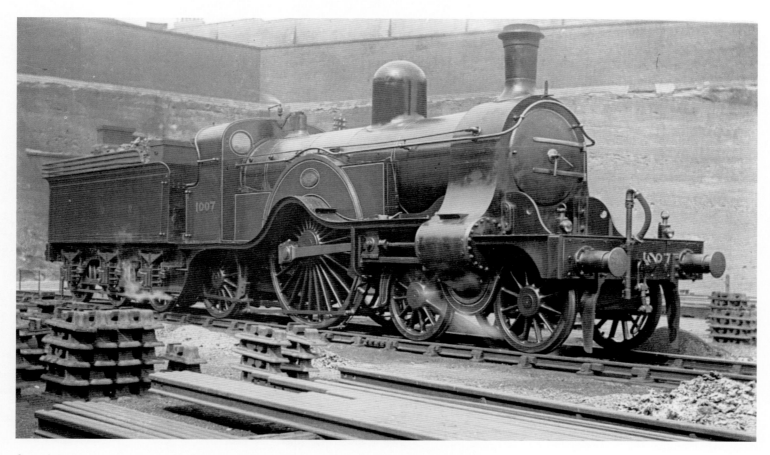

One of the later and larger Stirling 8ft singles No. 1007 here pictured at a joint GCR and GNR Nottingham Victoria station in 1911. The 4-2-2 is waiting between turns to work a semi fast service. The locomotive featured an Ivatt domed boiler, with this replacing the original Stirling domeless version, as well as a later pattern cab. By the end of the first decade of the twentieth century the 8ft singles were being cascaded on to less strenuous work on the GNR lines in Lincolnshire, where they worked cross country with lighter four- and six-wheeled carriage stock.

Although Patrick Stirling is best remembered for his 8ft singles, he was also responsible for other equally important locomotive designs. GNR E3 class 6ft 6in 2-4-0 tender locomotive, No. A291 was designed for mixed traffic work and is depicted at Nottingham Victoria station in August 1909 with a local service. Constructed by the Yorkshire Engine Company in Sheffield in 1868, the engine featured inside frames for the coupled wheels and outside frames for the leading axle. They were originally allocated to semi fast services on the main line from King's Cross to York. The 2-4-0 was cascaded to the GNR's duplicate list as A 291 under Henry Ivatt and was finally withdrawn in 1910.

Stirling GNR class 174, 5ft 2in Mineral 0-6-0 tender goods No. 197 at Basford in November 1911, with a local from Nottingham Victoria Station. The 0-6-0s were highly successful, with a total of 160, mostly constructed between 1871 and 1896 at Doncaster Works. They again featured Stirling's trademark domeless boiler and short open cabs. In 1892 two examples were re-built with new boilers with smaller fireboxes. No. 197 was withdrawn from service in 1916.

The GNR had a sizable fleet of saddle tank locomotives for shunting and pick up goods work. No. 857 was a Stirling example outshopped from Doncaster Works in 1892 for working over the widened lines near King's Cross. Examples were fitted with condensing gear. The GNR J15 class were long lived, with them becoming LNER class J52 and with the final example only withdrawn by BR, Eastern Region in March 1961. No. 857 is shown in the austere unlined grey livery of the Great War period.

The Stirling G2 Class 0-4-4 tanks were constructed at Doncaster works from 1872–81 for use on GNR suburban and branch line services. No. 533 was reconstructed in 1905 as a crane locomotive for use at Doncaster works, where it worked for many years. No. 533 was never allocated a stock number.

Henry Ivatt became locomotive superintendent of the GNR in 1895. He faced an urgent need for more powerful express passenger locomotives to haul the heavier main line trains and this resulted in the introduction of the Ivatt small boilered C2 'Atlantic' 4-4-2 locomotives in 1897, the first of this type of locomotive in Great Britain. The 'Klondikes' were well designed and powerful machines, hauling the principal expresses of the GNR until the introduction of Ivatt's larger C2 Atlantics in 1902. No. 258 is depicted at Nottingham Victoria Station while waiting for its next turn of duty in June 1912.

Large boilered Ivatt C2 Atlantic No. 1404 was constructed at Doncaster works in 1905 and had a long working life, not being withdrawn until July 1947. Initially, the performance of this class was found wanting, with Ivatt fitting them with a Schmidt superheater and piston valves from 1910. No. 1404 was photographed at Nottingham Victoria in 1912 and is painted in fully lined GNR apple green livery. These robust large boilered Atlantics were used on all principal LNER express services up until the late 1920s. The fitting of larger 32 element Robinson superheaters by Gresley when combined with piston valves, gave these capable machines a second new lease of life. For example, No. 4404 was 31 years old and not far off an overhaul, but still proved capable of keeping to time in July 1936 on a seventeen coach Up Edinburgh express when the usual Gresley A3 'Pacific' suffered a failure at Grantham on the East Coast Mainline.

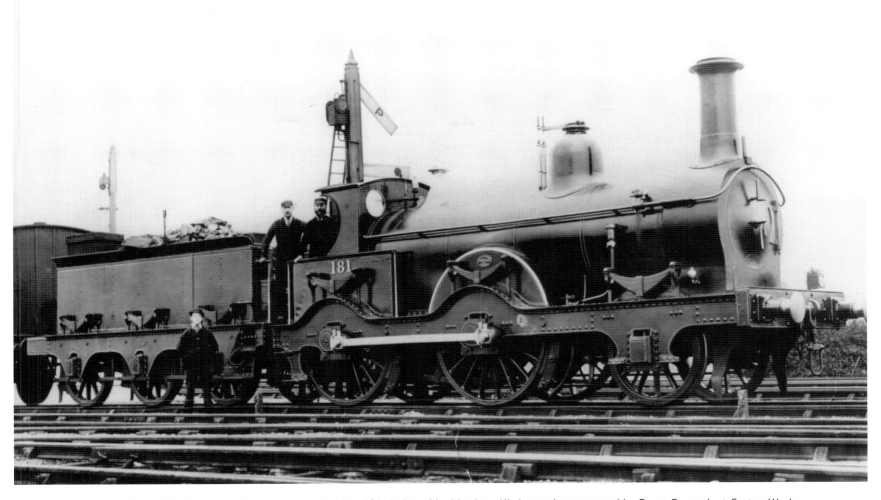

Midland Railway 170 Class 2-4-0 tender locomotive No. 181 designed by Matthew Kirtley and constructed by Beyer Peacock at Gorton Works, Manchester in 1869. These attractive workmanlike locomotives were used on passenger and fast perishable freight workings, being later reconstructed during the Johnson period with new boilers and cabs. Most lasted in traffic until the early decades of the twentieth century, when newer more powerful designs were introduced as trains became heavier.

Samuel Waite Johnson, a leading locomotive artist, designed some of the most elegant engines of the late Victorian period. The advent of effective steam sanding would enable a brief revival of the 'single' type; affording Johnson the opportunity to display at Derby Works what a supreme craftsman he was in his four designs of 4-2-2 'Spinners'. S Class 115 single No. 178 is captured on an express train at Nottingham c1905. Introduced in 1887, No. 178 was the last member of this class constructed at Derby in 1896 and featured a very large 7ft 9½in diameter driving wheel. However, on trains of 200 tons or less, they were still capable of 70mph or more on services into St Pancras from Nottingham and Leicester. After 1903, these locomotives were modified by his successor Richard Deeley, with the original elegant dish type Johnson smokebox door replaced by a less attractive, but more robust version with securing lugs around the circumference replacing the original central locking 'clock-hands'. They lasted through on principal passenger trains through the First World War, though they often needed a pilot locomotive. They were gradually withdrawn under the LMS between 1923 and 1932.

One of the last Johnson 4-4-2 'Spinners' to be constructed, No. 2602 is captured on shed awaiting its next turn of duty c1907. The exact origins of the name 'Spinner' are unclear, with it being claimed that the covered single drivers and absence of the usual visible valve gear and connecting rods, gave them the appearance that they 'spun' along almost effortlessly when at speed. Less charitably, it has also been claimed the large driving wheel still had a tendency to lose adhesion despite the fitting of steam sanding equipment. Sustained slipping on a wet rail or on steep gradients was still a problem. The fine lines of these beautiful late Victorian Derby express locomotives are clear, truly the work of an artist in Samuel Waite Johnson.

An example of Matthew Kirtley's standard outside frame Class 480 class 0-6-0 tender goods locomotives No. 2793. Introduced in 1863 for general goods traffic and trip working between goods yards, these locomotives had long lives and were constructed by both Derby Works and Dübs and Co of Glasgow. With robust frames and generous axle boxes, they were often to be seen double heading heavy coal and other goods workings heading into the capital. Successfully developed as a design, the last example was withdrawn by BR, London Midland Region in 1951. During the Great War the Railways Operations Division had a batch of these locomotives on the Western Front, one of which, No. 2717, was captured by the Germans, only later to be recaptured by the British.

One of Johnson's 1332 Class 0-4-0 Saddle Tanks No. 1507 photographed in 1907. These small useful shunting locomotives were first constructed at Derby Works in 1883.They lasted a long time, with the former 1506 surviving as Derby Works shunter and being allocated the BR, LMR number 41509. The first Midland design to be bestowed the esteemed title of 'Jinty', the last 0-4-0 saddle tank was not finally withdrawn until October 1949. The locomotive looks down at heel, with its brass numerals missing and its paint in a rundown condition. Note the two different patterns of driving wheels.

Midland Railway three cylinder compound locomotive No. 1044 at Kentish Town Shed c1914 in its original livery. The original Midland compounds were designed by S.W. Johnson and featured four 6ft 9in driving wheels. Walter Mackersie Smith was a gifted Scottish engineer whose work for the North Eastern Railway on both compounding and piston valves would lead him to patent a greatly improved system for compound working. This featured one large low pressure inside centre cylinder and two outside high pressure and smaller cylinders. An immediate success, both the Midland and the GCR would use Smith's patent, with this transforming the somewhat sluggish performance of Johnson's original version. The Midland Railway 1000 class were highly successful locomotives and featured on some of the Midland Railways fast Anglo-Scottish express services from London and on other principal passenger trains. Greatly improved under Johnson's successor Richard Deeley, No. 1044 is a fine example of a Smith patent compound and was constructed in 1907. After 1923, a further 195 were added to the original 45 examples under first LMS CME Henry Fowler and were classified as 4Ps under the LMS power classification scheme. The last example LMS Fowler No. 41168 was withdrawn on the 8 July 1961 under British Railways, London Midland Region.

Midland Railway Class 990 4-4-0 No. 724 seen at Kentish Town shed c1914. Originally designed by Samuel Johnson and later reconstructed by Richard Deeley, these useful express passenger tender locomotives featured two inside cylinders and were deployed on both express passenger trains and semi fast services. They were constructed between 1900 and 1905, with 73 of the 80 locomotives in the 700 class featuring superheating and Belpaire fireboxes. They were principally constructed by Deeley after 1907 for comparison with his recently modernised three-cylinder compound design and featured the same diameter 6ft 9in drivers. At the Midland's Leeds Wellington Station, 700 Compounds on services from St Pancras would give way to class 4P 990s on principle Anglo-Scottish Expresses for the steep climb over the steeply graded Settle and Carlisle Line They began to be withdrawn from the mid-1920s onwards as the small class of ten became increasingly non-standard among a sea of brand new Fowler LMS Compounds, with the last example withdrawn in February 1929.

A former London Tilbury & Southend Railway class 79 4-4-2 Radial tank No. 2111 designed by Thomas Whitelegg. This example is seen in Deeley reconstructed condition with a Midland style lug secured smokebox door and with former LT&SR name painted over. c1913. These successful tank locomotives were used on all former LT&SR passenger services from Fenchurch Street to Tilbury and Southend Central and classified under the Midland/LMS power classification as type 3P's. The class were later dispersed across the LMS system as more powerful 2-6-4 tanks became available, with the last example of the class withdrawn on 3 December 1960.

The Paget locomotive was a privately funded experimental project led by Cecil Paget, although the Midland Railway would end up paying for an impractical design, one which would end in the resignation of Richard Deeley as the Midland's Chief Mechanical Engineer. The locomotive was a unique outside frame 2-6-2 tender type, with eight inside cylinders and using the uniflow system and rotary sleeve valves. Oliver Bulleild's equally problematic double cab 0-6-0-0-6-0 'Leader' tank design of 1949 would also feature sleeve valves and would also prove equally unreliable with the valves becoming jammed or fracturing. The project was far from a success, with the locomotive breaking down frequently, though in keeping with the later 'Leader' class on occasions it could run well, attaining notably high speeds. Cecil Paget and Richard Mountford Deeley, the Midland Railways Chief Mechanical Engineer, did not see eye to eye on the design, with the capable Deeley resenting the aristocratic Paget's connections at board room level. Undermined, Deeley would walk into the design office one morning in late 1909 and have his brass name plate with his name unscrewed from the door. A big loss to locomotive design, Deeley was in the process of sketching his own design of large compound 4-6-0. He was never seen again at Derby. As for Sir Cecil Paget, during the Great War he would go on to lead the Railway Operations Department on the Western Front. Away on duties of national importance and with Paget no longer resident at Derby Works, the controversial multi-cylinder locomotive was quietly broken up for scrap in 1918, though it was technically not the property of the Midland Railway.

A John G. Robinson 11B 4-4-0 No. 1040 hauls an express on the Metropolitan & Great Central Joint line near Harrow c. 1908. These express passenger tender locomotives were introduced in 1901 for use on the most important passenger train services across the GCR system. They became LNER D9 class after the grouping in 1923 and were then largely concentrated on the Cheshire Lines Committee section and on services to York, Hull and Cleethorpes hauling semi fast and stopping train services. The class of forty was gradually withdrawn from the late 1930s, with the final example gone by July 1950.

The class 9N Pacific tanks were introduced in 1911 by John G. Robinson for suburban and semi fast passenger work. These purposeful 4-6-2 tank locomotives were used principally on GCR services from Marylebone and around Manchester Victoria, Sheffield Victoria and Nottingham Victoria on lucrative suburban and semi fast services. Later examples were fitted with a glazed enclosed cab. In elaborate GCR livery of Brunswick green and with Tuscan red frames, these large tank engines made an imposing and usually immaculate sight to behold. Under the LNER classification they became class A5. The final example was withdrawn on the 17 November 1960. An unidentified member of the class is captured hauling a suburban train on the Metropolitan & Great Central Joint line near Wembley c1912.

During the 1890s there was a shortage of locomotives for the nation's railways, with British locomotive manufacturers unable to supply enough locomotives for the home market. The demands of an expanding railway system right across a rapidly expanding British Empire, especially in India and Sub-Saharan Africa, where recently constructed British administered railways were booming and expanding, led to a shortage of rolling stock. A number of British railway companies were forced to order locomotives from American and German manufacturers, including the GCR, GNR, Midland, Cork Bandon & South Coast Railway in Ireland and the narrow gauge Lynton & Barnstaple Railway. An American Baldwin 'Yankie' Mogul 2-6-0 tender locomotive No. 956 is one of a batch of locomotives constructed in 1899 for the GCR as a stop gap solution to a shortage of goods locomotives as the new London Extension was opened in 1899. With bar frames and with distinctive American features, they made a most unusual sight on workings into Marylebone Goods depot. Designated as GCR class 15, each 2-6-0 cost only £2,600 to construct; with the Baldwin purchases replacing one for an order for conventional British outline Pollitt designed 0-6-0 tender goods locomotives. The American imports had relatively short lives, with the last withdrawn in 1915. This was not the last time however that the GCR would contemplate using American builds, with later in 1914 CME John G. Robinson developing a design for a massive conventional American outline 2-10-2 to work fast, heavy freights from Wath Marshalling Yard.

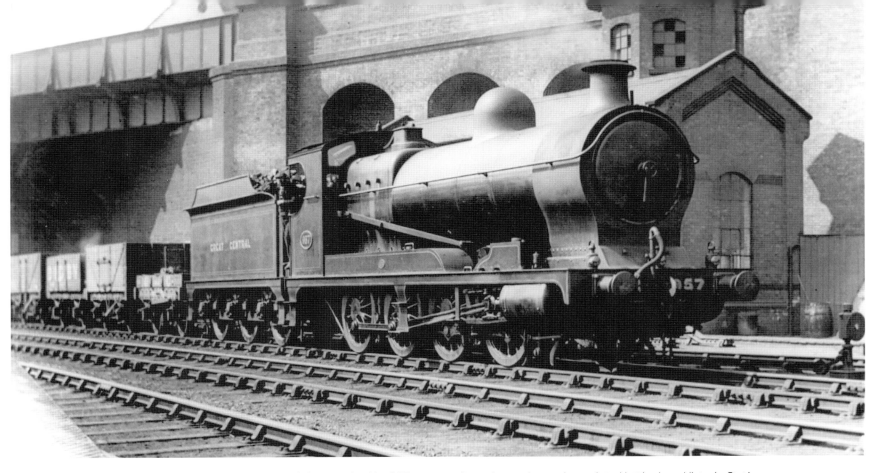

John G. Robinson class 8A 0-8-0 tender goods locomotive No. 957 emerges from the cutting and runs into Nottingham Victoria Station on a long, mixed goods train on 14 July 1911. These workman-like machines were first introduced in 1902 for heavy freight operations on the GCR and were Robinson's first venture into designing heavy freight locomotives. They were nicknamed 'Tinies' by the footplate crews. They were fitted with 21-element Robinson patent super heaters, which improved their steaming and coal and water consumption. Under the LNER, they became class Q41, while a number were reconstructed as class Q1 0-8-0 tanks in 1942/3 for heavy shunting in marshalling yards during Edward Thompson's tenure as CME. The last example in original tender form was withdrawn on 15 September 1958, with the last of the Thompson converted tank version gone by 1959.

A follow on from the 8A 0-8-0 tender heavy freight locomotives were the 8K 2-8-0 tender version with a greater range introduced in 1911. No. 394 is seen at Nottingham Victoria in ex works condition c1912. The John G. Robinson 8K class 2-8-0 tender heavy freight locomotives were well liked machines that could be relied upon to work long heavy trains in all conditions across the network. They became the 04 class in LNER days. During the First World War, the War Department ordered 521 of these powerful locomotives for the Western Front. They differed with the original 8Es by being fitted with steel fireboxes and Westinghouse air pumps for use with continental air braked rolling stock. After the war they were purchased by several British main line companies including the GWR, LNER and the LMS. A number of these locomotives were purchased for overseas railways, including China and Australia.

The 9C 0-6-2 tanks were introduced in 1892 and were designed by Thomas Parker for suburban and goods transfer work. No. 920 was constructed by the GCR in 1900 and is captured at work on station pilot duties at Nottingham Victoria on 14 July 1911. The locomotive has a Robinson chimney, replacing its original stove pipe chimney and also has the earlier plain GCR lettering on its side tanks. As with other GCR Gorton designs of the period, the smokebox door was secured by a central 'wheel' device to ensure a tight fit, with the adjacent Beyer Peacock Works at Gorton fitting a similar device to its exports for the Empire market and for domestic duties. Both Gorton Works directly influenced each other's designs. Classified N5 under the LNER scheme, the final members of the class not withdrawn until December 1960 under British Railways, Eastern Region.

John G. Robinson was another craftsman of the Edwardian period. A three-cylinder compound Atlantic 4-4-2 tender locomotives class 8D (LNER C5), No. 364 was constructed in 1906 and named *Lady Farringdon* in 1917. Along with his two-cylinder simple class 8B (LNER C4) 'Jersey Lilies', Robinson's Atlantics were among the most graceful of designs in a period blessed with many sumptuous on the eye creations. Both simple and compound versions headed the most important express trains on the GCR from 1903 onwards. No. 364 is seen at Nottingham Victoria in the centre road awaiting its next turn of duty. The final examples of GCR class 8D and 8E were withdrawn by 1947, with the final example of the former simple GCR 8B 'Jersey Lily' withdrawn as a class C4 on the 2 December 1950.

West of England Railways

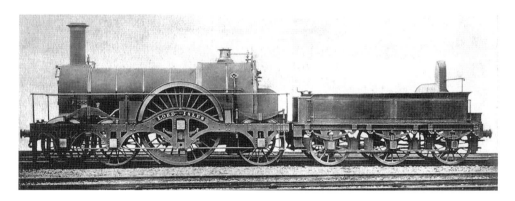

Broad gauge Iron Duke Class 4-2-2 single, *Lord of the Isles* was designed by Sir Daniel Gooch. The first examples of this then advanced design entered service in April 1846. Constructed by a new Swindon Works and Rothwell, Hick and Rothwell of Bolton, the class were a great success, with the type featuring strong double frames composed of wooden sections encased in twin metal plates. The final example was constructed in 1855, though the class was capable of being modernised, with new frames and boilers fitted after 1870. The three examples selected would become the basis of the 'Rover' class, the final great design to see service with the GWR until the end of the broad gauge in May 1892. Capable of prestigious feats of speed which put the then principal standard gauge companies to shame, the class would famously feature on the GWR's crack 'Flying Dutchman' express service from Paddington to Exeter, St Davids. *Lord of the Isles* was famously exhibited at the Great Exhibition in 1851 at the Crystal Palace in Hyde Park. After 1866, the imposing Lord of the Isles 4-2-2s were renamed as the 'Alma' class, with the original examples gradually withdrawn between December 1870 and June 1884. Although *Lord of the Isles* was originally set aside for preservation at Swindon; in 1906 on the orders of Locomotive Superintendent George Jackson Churchward, the giant engine, along with landmark Robert Stephenson 2-2-2 *North Star,* was broken up. There would be no room for nostalgia for a recently departed broad gauge on Churchward's rapidly modernising GWR.

Bristol & Exeter Railway broad gauge 4-2-2 express tender locomotive No. 2021. Formerly No. 43, the engine was designed by James Pearson and was re-constructed in 1871. No. 43 had originally been a most unusual giant 4-2-4 tank engine with a single 9ft driving wheel. Constructed in 1854 by Rothwell, Hick and Rothwell of Bolton, the type soon gained an unenviable reputation for rough riding on the South Devon Banks. They were used on fast and semi fast passenger trains from Bristol to Exeter from the 1870s until the end of the broad gauge in May 1892. The class were also to be seen running in the London Division of the GWR on excursion trains from the West of England, as well as on fast goods services. No. 2021 is pictured on shed, probably Bristol, Bath Road, the principal service shed for the Bristol and Exeter Railway in the city. Following amalgamation into a greater GWR in 1876, they were principally deployed west of Newton Abbott to Plymouth. All would be gone in the great cull of the last broad gauge rolling stock in May 1892.

There were twenty-four Renewals or Rover class 8ft 4-2-2 singles constructed between 1878 and 1888. They were probably the most famous broad gauge locomotive design, with the class dating from the Armstrong period and lasting in service under Locomotive Superintendent William Dean at Swindon. The Rover class headed the most important express passenger trains on the broad gauge and were often regularly timed at 70 or even at times 80mph on the fast run from London to Bristol and Exeter. Most of the class would survive in regular express service until the end of the broad gauge. Rebuilt from an example of the Lord of the Isles class originally dating from 1849, a new Rover class *Tornado* was shopped by Swindon Works with a Dean style cab featuring full side sheets in 1888.

William Dean continued with single drivers for standard gauge services. The Achilles class 3031 4-2-2s of 1891 were perhaps his finest work and were developed from his original class 3001 2-2-2s. Dean's original design suffered a spate of derailments, including a serious incident in Box Tunnel. A front bogie was inserted to cure the problem. The original thirty members of the 3001 class were subsequently rebuilt to 4-2-2 form. No. 3019 *Rover* is seen standing on shed c1906, with its crew looking proudly out from the cab. In 1900 an example would be fitted with a new Standard Number 2 taper boiler, with twelve examples subsequently converted as part of the Churchward revolution at Swindon. Though this may have improved their steaming, much of their outstanding overall elegance and sheer beauty was lost. Replaced on top link work with newer 4-6-0 and 4-4-0 tender locomotives, the final member of this celebrated class was withdrawn in December 1915.

William Dean would also introduce some fine 4-4-0 tender locomotives in the form of the 3252 Duke class of 1896. These versatile locomotives headed some of the most important trains on the GWR when first introduced and continued in regular service until the late 1940s, with the final example only withdrawn under British Railways, Western Region in July 1951. No. 3263 *Sir Lancelot* is seen at Wellington with a ballast train in 1905.

George Jackson Churchward had succeeded Dean as locomotive superintendent at the GWR's Swindon Works in 1902. He was above all responsible for a revolution in standardisation, producing by 1921 a modern fleet of world class locomotives. One of his early 2-6-2 Prairie tanks No. 3120, the first in the 3120 class, was constructed for suburban work in the London Division of the GWR in 1905. These useful and well-designed locomotives proved would be further developed in both small and large form until the 1930s under Churchward's successor as CME, Charles B. Collett.

GWR City class 3700 4-4-0 3433 *City of Bath* photographed in original condition without top feed around the safety valve bonnet and coupled to a Dean style tender c1904. Constructed in May 1903, the class were a transitionary express passenger designed on the cusp of the Dean and Churchward eras at Swindon. One was based on the successful trial fitting of a new design large domeless prototype Standard Number 4 boiler to a member of the 'Atbara' class 4-4-0s in 1902. The double framed chassis with its prominent outside cranks was pure Dean, along with the two inside cylinders, inside Stephenson valve gear and slide valves. Yet the boiler barrel, with its gentle taper and a large Belpaire firebox; stood in sharp contrast with the rest and hinted at far greater things to come with a fresh broom at Swindon Works under the inimitable George Jackson Churchward. The class featured 6ft 8½in diameter driving wheels and were clearly capable of spurts of high speed given the legendary exploits of another member of the class 3440 *City of Truro* down Wellington Bank on 9 May 1904 with the great driver Moses W. Clements at the regulator. Whether 100mph was actually achieved remains a subject of fierce debate to this day, yet somewhat misses the point as the City class as a whole hinted at far greater and faster things to come on a rapidly modernising standard gauge only GWR. *City of Bath* was renumbered in 1912 and fitted after 1908 with a superheater, an extended longer smokebox to accommodate the device, top feed for boiler water supply and finally on the eve of the First World War, modern piston valves. These additions would significantly change the appearance of this celebrated class, with *City of Bath* withdrawn in May 1931.

No. 3297 *Earl Cawdor* was a one-off member of the 4100 Badminton 4-4-0 class. The locomotive was constructed in May 1898 at Swindon and was quite unlike any other GWR outside frame 4-4-0, being fitted in 1903 with a large round top boiler and roomy enclosed cab similar to those fitted to contemporary GER and NER designs. The one off 4-4-0 was one of Churchward's experiments in locomotive design during the transition period from Dean, with a radical Churchward trialling an alternative to his more usual design of conical or taper boiler and Belpaire firebox. The work of Churchward's Chief Assistant, F.G. Wright, the round top boiler was not deemed worthy of further development. *Earl Cawdor* was fitted with a more conventional Standard Number 4 boiler in October 1906 with all members of the 4100 withdrawn by 1931.

GWR class 29xx No. 2908 *Lady of Quality* was constructed in May 1906 and was originally unnamed. The engine is shown as running with top feed fitted to its Standard Number 1 boiler after. The fitting of top feed meant water was introduced into the boiler via a series of sloping internal trays, with this increasing boiler life. No. 2908 was fitted with a superheater in April 1911, outside steam pipes in December 1935 and was finally withdrawn under British Railways, Western Region in December 1950. George Jackson Churchward would look for inspiration at the latest ideas from home and abroad, most notably from North America with regard to taper boilers, with Churchward a personal friend of the Pennsylvania Railroad's CME Alfred Wolcott Gibbs. With an open-minded design philosophy, he would combine practical hands-on workshop experience gained initially on the South Devon Railway and later at Swindon, mathematics and a rigorous scientific approach to observing and collating actual running data from his new breed of Swindon two- and four-cylinder taper boiler designs. As part of this, the Dean designed Dynamometer car and Churchward's Swindon Test Plant of 1904 based on the original 'Pennsy's Altoona version; would both play an important role in enabling Churchward to ascertain optimum performance right across his emerging range of modern standardised locomotives. His 'Saint' design was a direct product of this painstaking and patient design philosophy, being developed from February 1902, with Churchward eventually producing the first truly modern two cylinder 4-6-0 design in the United Kingdom. Whereas other railways – notably the L&SWR and Caledonian – would also introduce large 4-6-0 designs, these were in effect only stretched 4-4-0s rather than an attempt to produce a genuine bespoke ten wheel design. Eventually married to high temperature superheating under William Stanier on the LMS, Churchward had laid the ground for the classic British 4-6-0, with this leading to the GWR's Hall, Manor, Grange, Modified Hall and County classes, the LMS classic 'Black Five' and finally the often overlooked and underrated BR Standard class 5. The significance of Churchward's original Swindon design in British locomotive history cannot be underestimated.

Churchward was impressed by the designs of Alfred de Glenn, a gifted London born engineer, whose work for the French Société Alsacienne de Constructions Mécaniques would help revolutionise French railway working at the turn of the nineteenth century. De Glenn was undoubtedly one of the leading figures in the development of the modern steam locomotive of the twentieth century. Noting their superb construction and economy in operation, Churchward ordered three de Glenn Compound Atlantic locomotives of differing designs for experiments on the GWR. They were divided drive four- cylinder locomotives, with the low pressure inside cylinders driving the front driving axle and the outside high pressure cylinders the rear drivers. They were appropriately named, 102 *La France*, seen here,103 *Precedent* and 104 *Alliance*. Delivered in 1903, they originally sported an overall black livery not dissimilar to that of the L&NWR. The experiments failed to prove the benefits of compounding over a modern 'simple' design, with Churchward specially adapting a former 4-6-0 171 *Albion* to 4-4-2 condition for the trials. The non-standard French trio were fitted with Swindon Standard Number 1 boilers after 1916, while the earlier black livery was soon replaced in 1906 by the more usual GWR 'Bronze' Green. However, the de Glenn bogie was a superb design, a type which its system of supporting cups and secondary bolster would be fitted with little modification to a generation of modern GWR, LMS and BR Standard designs. Significantly Churchward's advanced 'simple' four cylinder 4000 '*Star*' class 4-6-0's of 1906 would copy the De Glenn Atlantics' divided drive, as would later Collett GWR four cylinder 4-6-0 thoroughbreds in the 4073 '*Castle*' class of 1923 and 6000 '*King*' class of 1927. The last De Glenn Atlantic was withdrawn in October 1926. No.102 *La France* is pictured at Bath station c1906 with an express passenger service.

GWR 'Star' class four cylinder class 4000 No. 4055 *Princess Sophia* as fitted with top feed c1914. The next development in express passenger designs would see Churchward successfully combine the divided drive, Walschaerts valve gear, four cylinders, and improved design of de Glenn bogie of the French Atlantics, with his Standard Number 1 boiler of the Saint class, with this pressed to as much as 225psi. A subtle, careful mix of best British, French, Belgian and American traditions, Churchward had produced a genuine masterpiece, one which would be subsequently developed under Charles B. Collett into the famous Castle and King class four-cylinder 4-6-0's and would go on to see out steam on British Rail, Western Region in 1965. No. 4055 was constructed in July 1914 and was allocated initially to old Oak Common Shed in West London, Working principle express services to Bristol Temple Meads, Plymouth, North Road Wolverhampton. Low Level and Birmingham, Snow Hill, the engine was fitted with external steam pipes in May 1945 and withdrawn from Swindon shed in 1951.

The GWR class 927 0-6-0 tender goods locomotives were specially designed by Joseph Armstrong to haul heavy trains carrying best steam coal from South Wales to Birkenhead Woodside in order to replenish the bunkers of Cunard and Canadian Pacific trans-Atlantic ocean liners calling at the Port of Liverpool. With the first of the class constructed at Swindon in 1874, they were a distinctive design, featuring double frames and outside cranks. They were also fitted with notably small cabs which gave little real protection to crews in bad weather or in particular when traversing the sulphurous 4-mile-long Severn Tunnel. No. 945 is captured between such onerous heavy duties.

Another notable William Dean tank design was the 2-4-0 Metro Tank, a development of Joseph Armstrong's already successful design of 1869. Dean's class 455 was an enlarged version and used on London suburban services. For working through services from Paddington Bishop's Road to Moorgate Street over the Metropolitan Railway, they were fitted with obligatory condensing apparatus. The class was also used on Smithfield meat train, which ran through from Acton Yard to Farringdon for Smithfield Market in the City of London. These useful and long-lived tanks were later cascaded to work on branch lines across the GWR system, with the last not being withdrawn from South Wales until 28 January 1949 by British Railways, Western Region, Condenser fitted No. 3582 simmers in the yard of a new Old Oak Common Shed c1910.

The Somerset & Dorset Joint Railway linking Bath, Green Park with Bournemouth West was one of Britain's most celebrated rural cross-country lines. The Joint Company began life as two separate railways, the Somerset Central and the Dorset Central. These amalgamated and were then taken over jointly in 1875 by the Midland Railway and the L&SWR. After the grouping in 1923 it became the joint property of the LMS and Southern Railway, with the wandering secondary route finally closing under British Rail, Western Region auspices on the 7 March 1966. Constructed at Derby in 1891, a Samuel Johnson designed 4-4-0 tender locomotive No. 18 is seen on a passenger train c1900. The S&D locomotives were from 1875 to the early 1930s painted in an elegant rendering of lined Prussian blue, with the goods locomotives being painted black. The separate S&D fleet of engines were maintained at the Company's small works at Highbridge, with later Derby Works undertaking heavy overhauls and repairs after the works closed in May 1930.

0-6-0 tender goods No. 23 was constructed by John Fowler and Joint Railway. No. 23 is seen as reconstructed by Samuel Johnson and is coupled to a long goods train c1895. Note the rounded locomotive cab and the proud train crew wearing bowler hats.

An example of a Somerset & Dorset tank locomotive. No. 28A was originally a 2-4-0 tank saddle tank in 1861 constructed by George England at Hatcham Iron Works, New Cross London and was later reconstructed under S.W. Johnson as a side tank. The locomotive is photographed in work shop grey and in its later form with standard Midland Railway fittings.

Index